Deaf Children in Public Schools

Ceil Lucas, General Editor

Deaf Children in Public Schools

Placement, Context, and Consequences

Claire L. Ramsey

GALLAUDET UNIVERSITY PRESS

Washington, D.C.

Sociolinguistics in Deaf Communities

A Series Edited by Ceil Lucas

Gallaudet University Press

Washington, D.C. 20002

ISBN 1–56368–062–9

ISSN 1080–5494

Cover design by Dorothy Wachtenheim

Interior design by Richard Hendel

Composition by Graphic Composition, Inc.

Classroom models for cover photograph: Lianna Rogers, Tony Green, Andrea Wukitsch, Ms. Doris Schwarz, and Andrew Donald

Cover photograph taken by Chun Louie

∞ The paper used in this publication meets the minimum requirements of American National Standard for Information Sciences—Permanence of Paper for Printed Library Materials, ANSI Z39.48–1984.

for
Larry Whitson

Contents

Editor's Introduction

This third volume in the Sociolinguistics in Deaf Communities series represents a departure from the previous format of a collection of papers. What is contained here is the work of one person, but it is a work that brings together the different concerns of sociolinguistics—from the structure and use of language, language policy and planning, and discourse to bilingualism, language contact, and language attitudes.

This is a book about the use of language in deaf education, an issue that, at its core, is essentially sociolinguistic in nature. It is a sociolinguistic issue because it involves the choice of language that will be used as the medium of instruction for Deaf children; it is sociolinguistic because it concerns the contact of distinct languages and the outcomes of this contact; and it is sociolinguistic because it has direct bearing on users of language, be they children, parents, administrators, or teachers. This volume provides a concise example of what we mean by "sociolinguistics in Deaf communities;" that is, a picture of the place where language structure and language users meet.

Dr. Claire Ramsey began the research reported here for a dissertation, the writing of which was supported by a fellowship from the Spencer Foundation. Her efforts were recognized as Dissertation of the Year in the University of California, Berkeley, Graduate School of Education (1993). The dissertation also received honors for scholarship from the International Reading Association in 1994 and was recognized as Dissertation of the Year by Division G (Social Context of Education) of the American Educational Research Association (AERA). We are very fortunate to be able to offer it as a part of this series.

I am grateful to my old friend and colleague Dr. Claire Ramsey for contributing to the series and to the members of the editorial advisory board for their diligence in reviewing papers. And as always, I am grateful to Ivey Pittle Wallace, Managing Editor of Gallaudet University Press, for her continuing hard work and sense of humor.

Ceil Lucas
Washington, D.C.

Preface

I was a nervous elementary schoolgirl the first time around, and I often boarded that big yellow schoolbus with a knot in my stomach. I was never sure what I would suffer that day at the hands of my teachers, who were probably completely professional, well meaning, and competent, but who often seemed like omnipotent savages to me. So many of the rules of school were implicit. For many of us, public schools are mysterious places structured by rules that are learned best after breaking them. I never wanted to break a school or classroom rule, but at the same time, I was never good at figuring them out.

Attending second grade all over again as an adult was only a little bit easier. Almost every day, as I parked near Aspen School, the familiar "school stomachache" visited me again. I signed on for another year of elementary school, though, for two reasons—I needed to gather data so I could write a dissertation, and I needed to revisit elementary school and problematize its oddities so that I could make sense of a school phenomenon that puzzled me. This phenomenon is called "mainstreaming deaf children." I did my research using ethnographic methods because I wanted to see mainstreaming and self-contained classes from the participants' viewpoints. It was a frightening and thrilling year in the field.

I can never repay my debt to Robbie, Tom, Paul, and their parents, or to Ms. Roberts, Ms. Adams, Mrs. Hart, and Mrs. Rogers for graciously welcoming me into their lives at Aspen School. I am certain I owe a large cosmic debt to these wonderful women and boys, who I subjected to many hours of videotaping.

I am grateful to Herb Simons and Anne Haas Dyson, who served as members of my dissertation committee at the University of California at Berkeley and who continue to extend their friendship. At the University of California at San Diego I had the benefit of doing research with Carol Padden and Tom Humphries, which helped me find a direction for my work. I thank Ceil Lucas of Gallaudet University for many years of friendship and for encouraging me to believe that a wider audience would find my research interesting. Kelly Stack, Nina Ramsey, and Carol Padden generously loaned me video equipment during the study, for which I am grateful.

By a stroke of genetic luck, I inherited not only deep and tenacious curiosity but a refined sense of the ridiculous. For this, and for many years of patient if mystified support, I thank James Ramsey, Suzanne E. Ramsey, Nina Ramsey, and Carol Docksteader. Finally, I am grateful to the Spencer Foundation for a Dissertation Year Fellowship and for very generous continuing support of my research.

Then you will do your duty, for it is not necessary to be dubbed a knight to engage in battles such as these.

—Miguel de Cervantes, *Don Quixote*

Chapter 1

Deaf Children and Appropriate

Contexts for Education

While sitting in my first sign language class in the basement of a speech and hearing clinic many years ago, I never dreamed I would eventually spend much of my adult time in elementary classrooms with deaf children. Yet classrooms for deaf students have become my workplace as a researcher. In the mid-1980s I found myself in possession of a Comprehensive Skills Certificate from the Registry of Interpreters for the Deaf (RID), a master's degree in linguistics from Gallaudet University, and a job in an elementary school "mainstreaming program" for deaf children. In many ways, this program was an exotic place, and I felt very much the foreign visitor surrounded by a new locale and its inhabitants. This seemingly commonplace job as an instructional assistant for deaf children offered glimpses of many mystifying practices. The deaf children I worked with were sent to several different school settings each day, from their small and diverse (two second-graders, two third-graders, one sixth-grader) self-contained class to their mainstreaming class, to recess, lunch, PE, and art class with hearing children. Observing the deaf children in these settings, I wondered about their learning and development and the ways communication at school might contribute to or constrain their growth. In particular, although I was familiar with the logic behind "placement" options for deaf students, I had many questions about the organizational details of the classrooms the deaf students were sent to. My subsequent research program has developed from these questions about elementary education for deaf children in integrated and self-contained classes. Specifically, I ask how educational placements function as contexts for deaf children's learning.

Over the years, the situated nature of learning and development have become very clear to me. My descriptions of schooling contexts focus on children as social beings, on schools as sites where group life dominates and takes on great importance, and on interaction with others as the driving force in learning and development. Neither deaf nor hearing children can develop in isolation from others, nor do they develop in neutral settings. Contexts for learning (i.e., schools) are arranged by adults who assemble groups of children to learn together under a teacher's direction. For many deaf children for whom signing is their primary language, the contexts of schooling, and the people they interact with there (deaf and hearing peers, teachers, and interpreters) play a critical role in their lives, especially if they return to families and neighborhoods where there are few signers.

This book addresses both theoretical and strategic questions. The durability of programs for deaf and hard of hearing students in public schools makes it imperative to examine everyday practices and language use in these settings, where most young deaf children now receive their elementary education. There are inexcusable gaps in our knowledge of the linguistic and social contexts of deaf education and of the communicative processes at work in these settings. Critically, we also lack knowledge about the protagonists in deaf education, that is, deaf children themselves.

To write the detailed account that follows, I once again visited an elementary school, which I call "Aspen School." This time I did not fill the easy-to-define niche of instructional assistant. Rather, I occupied the more vague role of the "participant observer," which made me not only an observer in the classroom but an observed participant as well. Three deaf, signing second graders—Tom, Robbie, and Paul—the adults who taught them, as well as the children's parents, kept their eyes on me and permitted me an almost undreamed of luxury for a researcher: a school year of visiting time with very few constraints and blanket permission to videotape ongoing classroom life.

The purpose of the study was to uncover the institutional forces that identified educational placements for deaf children and to describe the learning contexts that resulted in the deaf and hard of hearing program at Aspen School. Accordingly, the research was structured by questions about the deaf children's everyday life at school. Tom's, Robbie's, and Paul's schooling unfolded in two different locations: a regular second-grade classroom where the deaf students were mainstreamed with hearing students, and a self-contained classroom for deaf and hard of hearing students. Different sets of beliefs about the deaf children's most crucial needs structured each setting. In the mainstreaming classroom they were defined as children who merely needed their civil right to educational access ensured. In contrast, in the self-contained classroom, they were regarded as children who needed a specific kind of teaching because they were deaf. Under these circumstances, the teacher in the mainstreaming class could not realistically hold educational goals for the deaf students, since the children were there not for educational reasons but in order to accomplish legal goals. The teachers in the self-contained classroom, on the other hand, were working toward educational goals. They expected the deaf students to improve their face-to-face communicative competence, acquire and practice basic literacy skills, and learn how to be students who are deaf.

The theme of this book is that educational placements and learning contexts are not the same phenomena and do not necessarily overlap. This observation is not a new one. Concerns about the ability of local public schools to meet deaf students' specific educational needs have been expressed by both general educators and teachers of the deaf as well as by deaf adults since the mid-70s, when it appeared that integrated classrooms would become the primary educational settings for deaf students. The research builds upon and goes beyond these concerns to document a mainstreaming program that is typical in many ways, especially in the tension and confusion that accompanied the complex problems of everyday school practice.

LEARNING: THE SOCIAL FACTOR

Although this book is about deaf students and their education, the questions discussed are firmly grounded in broader theories of human development. For all children, teaching and learning have powerful social roots. To understand the general developmental trajectories of deaf children, we do not need to devise new theories that apply to deaf children alone. Without diminishing the critical educational implications of deafness in early childhood, I maintain that deaf children, since they are human children, have many developmental needs that are not different from those of hearing children. Primarily, they need opportunities to use language to engage with others. These occasions must be embedded in comprehensible social contexts where there are other children and adults who share the language and who can help make the world intelligible. The generally low school achievement of deaf children may have many sources, but from my observation, it is often imposed upon normally intelligent deaf children by well-meaning educators who place them in settings where they cannot interact meaningfully with others and thus cannot learn and develop.

Lev Vygotsky's (1962, 1978) "sociohistorical" theory is built on claims about the social origins of the mind, including the role of interaction with others in learning and development. Vygotsky also considered the role of culture, especially as it is encoded in language, as a mediator of learning and development. From this perspective, the unit of analysis, or the focus of interest, is not the individual child and his or her growing accumulation of achievements. Rather, sociohistorical theorists look at developing children as members of groups with histories and cultures that structure and help to organize their lives. Because this point of view directs attention to language use, interaction, and the organization of learning contexts, it provides a fruitful set of tools for examining classrooms, settings where culture is the organizer, where culture emerges, and where learning and development take place.

Although it is conventional to focus on the disability of deaf children, their inability to hear, an alternative perspective is needed. At a time when the existence of a Deaf culture is recognized and when the bilingual realities of Deaf people's lives are widely accepted, we need a realistic view of deaf children. Such a concept would reconcile their biological attribute of not hearing with the need that all children have to learn and grow among people with whom they can fully interact. The theoretical discussion that follows constructs a sociohistorical framework to suggest a general way to reconcile biology and culture in education for deaf children. Rather than using a series of placements, education for deaf students must be considered in contexts where learning and development are either fostered or impeded.

Three ideas are paramount in this discussion. First, in educational settings, language use must be made problematic. That is, we cannot look through language as if it were an invisible or a neutral medium. We must focus on it in order to reveal the processes by which it succeeds or fails in the classroom. Second, language is more than a system for constructing well-formed utterances. In order to learn, children need repeated and intelligible interaction with other people who are users of a shared language with a history. Simply producing well-constructed sentences is not sufficient. Third, interaction creates avenues for mediating activities. That is, through social intercourse, maturing children harness cultural tools, their language acquisition unfolds, and their knowledge of the world is accumulated and interpreted. Importantly, in surroundings organized for development and learning, language and interaction allow children to use the tools that their culture hands down to them to think, to learn about and to manipulate symbol systems, and to become a member not only of their social group but also of the symbol-using human species.

Language in the Classroom

Most schooling activities are shaped by language as it is used in classrooms. Cazden (1988) argues that classroom communication is "a problematic medium that cannot be ignored as transparent by anyone interested in teaching and learning" (p. 3). She points out that language is the medium through which most teaching flows and the means by which students demonstrate what they have learned. Cazden recognizes that language and social identity are strongly linked and that both students and teachers bring social and linguistic identities to the classroom. These may imply differences in forms of language and in the ways language is used at school. In turn, these variations can affect learning, teaching, and evaluation, including what counts as knowledge.

For all the pedagogical attention devoted to media of communication in deaf education, the actual functions, successes, or failures of language used in classroom settings for deaf children have long been transparent to many practitioners and researchers. Yet, educational surroundings for deaf children are social and linguistic contexts characterized by issues of control and of social identity. Since, in theory, language is the medium that structures teaching and learning, then language use is a reasonable place to investigate the sources of problems and successes in deaf students' schooling.

Access to Intelligible Interaction

Much of the education of deaf children aims to remediate their perceived abnormality. It is not uncommon to hear teachers and parents of deaf students express their desire to help deaf children become as "normal" as possible. Accordingly, I work from a basic framework that hypothesizes how development in young human beings proceeds. Presumably, developing children who are deaf need fine-tuned support for their specific needs. I argue that the medium for such assistance should be a natural human language that is signed rather than spoken. However, in more fundamental ways, deaf children's needs may not be so different from those of children in general.

My questions about the contexts of deaf education emphasize interaction through language. Two related notions inform my questions. First, language is a complex, abstract system of meanings, forms, rules, and functions that have developed over time among a community of users; as such, it is much more than a set of well-formed utterances. Second, children cannot and do not develop this complex system completely on their own. Clearly, they need access to others who know how to use the language conventionally in order to foster their own innate potential for linguistic competence.

This framework differs somewhat from beliefs underlying language policies in deaf education. In fact, a more common definition of language development takes well-formedness of utterances as the primary evidence of growing competence. A popular "input-output" theory of language development in deaf children is presented in materials describing Signing Exact English (SEE), a pedagogical system of signing that relies upon a signed representation of each morpheme of English (e.g., Gustason et al. 1972). Deaf children who receive SEE input, it is said, will emulate it and eventually produce well-structured English output. In this scheme, input provides models of language, and output produces evidence of language development. From this input, deaf children will extract sufficient knowledge of English to enable them to learn to read and write English. Nevertheless, there is compelling evidence that this is not the case when SEE is employed (Stack 1996; Supalla 1986). In addition, when SEE-signing children also happen to be proficient readers, there is little understanding of the role SEE has played in their development of English print literacy. Despite the mixed empirical base, American educators of deaf students have long held that deaf children must receive relatively mechanistic language input in order to learn.

In contrast, I contend that putting language to purposeful social and cognitive use constitutes and promotes language development in children, whether they live among users of English, Spanish, or ASL (Halliday 1975; Nelson 1985). Under typical circumstances, children do not acquire language solely in order to utter grammatical sentences. Rather, as they communicate with those around them, processes of language acquisition unfold, and children come to understand and participate in the social world they inhabit with others. Through their own physical and social actions in familiar settings with familiar people whose language is intelligible to them, developing children harness the power of their human birthright: their built-in ability to acquire language rapidly, their immense capacity to learn, and their wide range of symbolic capabilities. Many adults have observed children cracking the code of language, building on what they know as they develop new knowledge, and generally exploiting their ability to learn how language works from their interactions with others.

Normal language development in childhood is accomplished not through formal instruction but through everyday life. Children do not think like adults (Donaldson 1978), nor are they able immediately to regard language as an object as adults do (Stubbs 1980; Ferreiro and Teberosky 1982). The paradox of language development is that internal cognitive and symbolic processes are initiated and supported in local social contexts that in turn bring children into contact with the broad knowledge of their culture's conventions of language forms and uses. These internal, and initially very local, processes lead to cultural understanding and allow developing children to become competent members of their speech community. An educational overemphasis on syntactically correct utterances strips from language its power to help children evolve into symbol-seeking and symbol-manipulating members of social and cultural groups.

As noted, children cannot bring about their development completely on their own. In Vygotskyan terms, language is the medium through which learning happens. Vygotsky (1978) makes the strong claim that learning "awakens a variety of internal developmental processes that are able to operate only when the child is interacting with people in his environment and in cooperation with his peers" (p. 90). This implies that, without interaction through language, development will be problematic.

This broad developmental framework can inform observations of deaf children precisely because the reality of their young, unfolding lives contrasts sharply with that of hearing children. The key fact is that hearing children acquire language naturally through the routines of early life. Most deaf children, even though they share the developmental potential of hearing children, generally do not. It is not unusual for deaf children to receive direct and explicit language instruction in their first language in educational settings. Rather than learning language as they grow into competent membership in a social group, they are expected to develop language virtually alone, via direct instruction; in fact, Furth (1973) claims that "deaf children derive a considerable amount of ego strength from the simple fact that they are the originators and masters of their symbolic life to a much greater extent than hearing children" (p. 73). This claim implies that there is some benefit to going it alone, a notion that classroom experience with deaf children certainly invalidates.

To complicate matters, most deaf children are expected to acquire a spoken language first—perhaps English—despite the fact that they are acutely detached from the English-speaking community and may never be able to join it fully and that a signing community exists that could provide access to a natural language. Thus, deaf children's attempts at first language acquisition and early literacy development often lack the support of intelligible interaction, the very processes that unlock their inner symbolic power as well as afford admission to a social world.

Mediating Activities in Development

The processes by which social settings and interaction with others foster intellectual, linguistic, and literacy growth are built upon mediation, a central concept in Vygotskyan accounts of learning and development. *Mediation* is the exploitation of intermediate, indirect "tools" that enable individuals to engage with their context, both the immediate, local setting (e.g., a classroom) and the historical and cultural features transmitted by that setting (e.g., in American schools, the use of English, the focus on English literacy, the organization of space and equipment as well as the teacher's pedagogical methods).

Children's efforts to learn depend on external supports, tools, and objects—both material and symbolic. For example, during their school writing activities, the children I studied relied not only on material tools like crayons, scissors, pencils, marking pens, and lined paper but also on external symbolic tools. Examples of the latter include alphabetized lists of words on classroom bulletin boards, calendars, classmates' fingerspelling and written texts, entries in their own journals used as lexicons or glossaries, and fingerspelling and ASL signed to themselves. In this theoretical framework, the child's processes of seeking support from various sources constitute mediating activities that employ these tools.

Hypothetically, as development proceeds, activities that begin as social—between a child and her peers and teachers, for example—eventually become internalized. The social processes by which young deaf writers might seek help, figure out equivalent meanings between signs and printed words, and encode those meanings in writing will be reformed, based on their mediating activities, and internalized. Rather than forming a question about composing a sentence and asking an adult, in theory, through practice and supported participation in this activity, the child will become able to compose sentences on her own, with fluency and automaticity that increase with practice.

Vygotsky describes internalization as a lengthy series of transitions through which the external—activities, conversations, and interactions among people—becomes reconstructed and internal. Vygotsky's (1978) stance is that "higher mental functions"—the cognitive and symbolic abilities and the strategies for learning that we expect children to acquire in school—originate as relations between people. In other terms, complex cognitive activities develop through participation in culturally organized interactions. Under typical circumstances of development, these interactions occur when adults or more experienced peers engage children through socially constructed symbol systems (e.g., a shared language).

The unit of analysis for observing these supported and mediated transformations is "the-individual-acting-with-mediational-means" (Wertsch 1989). For example, if we want to observe the phenomenon of early literacy using this theory as a guide, we will not be satisfied with a test score or a demonstration of what the individual child can do with a book. Rather, we would observe a child, taking into consideration his or her emerging or established communicative competence, engaging in a literacy activity with adult and peer interlocutors. We would be especially interested in the ways the child adapts to challenges and the kinds of assistance others provide. We would also pay close attention to the functions for which the child uses language (addressed to others or subtly addressed to herself) when tackling difficult activities. Many school tasks, especially literacy tasks, require children to develop conscious awareness of what they are doing, reflectiveness about what they have done, and control of simultaneously executed complex tasks (e.g., transforming a thought into a sentence, spelling the words, adhering to rules of grammar as well as the conventions of English print, and possibly demonstrating to a teacher that the task has been accomplished). For these critical activities, language is the primary medium that focuses mental orientation and clarifies conscious understanding. Without language competence and intelligible interlocutors to use as tools, children would find it almost impossible to participate in the most commonplace school tasks.

This complex theoretical perspective, where language enjoys a privileged position as the most powerful mediating tool, presents a new perspective on development and learning among deaf children. Because communication plays a primary role in children's intellectual and linguistic progress, we have only to look at the generations of American deaf schoolchildren and their struggles toward literacy to see what is missing. Unhappily, many deaf American children do not have early or complete access to a natural language and therefore cannot make use of its mediating powers for their learning and development. These children have limited or only indirect access to English because they cannot hear speech. They usually have no access to ASL because it is generally not used in mainstream classrooms, is not taught to most deaf children, and is not available to them in childhood because deaf adults are not present in elementary education programs (Woodward et al., 1988). At least one source of the consistent problems deaf children experience at school may not be their inadequate English proficiency or their hearing deficit but a more profound lack of access to a fully elaborated, culturally living symbol system that they can exploit to further their activities with the world and with other people.

THREE QUESTIONS

This theoretical perspective raised three questions that are critical topics in the education of deaf and hard of hearing students. The research reported here provides data that may eventually lead to theoretically grounded practical answers. Researchers and progressive educators of deaf and hard of hearing students need to be prepared to answer these questions.

Why Does Intelligible Language Matter?

In theoretical terms, language is the primary mediating tool for learning and for development. Language allows us to exploit our human abilities to learn and to think. Because language is at the core of human association, it gives us access to the people who are around us now and to those with whom we will interact in the future. If, for some reason, children do not have complete and intelligible access to their group's language, they will not be able to use its mediating power in their personal growth, nor will they be afforded direct, unimpeded contact with that language's community of users and their cultural history.

Why Study the Social Life of Children Instead of Measuring
Individual Achievement? Or, Why Does Interaction Matter?

To restate Vygotsky's claim, it is only through interaction with others, or what he views as "learning," that developmental processes can unfold. Through interaction, children have access to the processes by which people think, solve problems, discover new knowledge, and build on previously attained knowledge. During interaction with others, children can be both recipients and agents; they can ask for and receive assistance from others; and they can also provide assistance to others.

What Is a Context? Why Do Contexts Matter?

The scope of the present theoretical framework demands that we go beyond the idea of placement of children in educational environments (a topic discussed further in chapter 2). This book examines contexts for deaf children's learning. The term *context* is used to reflect the complexity of settings designed for teaching and learning.

Cole and Cole (1993) suggest that a context is not a simple location but "is more properly thought of as a relationship between behavior, the event of which the behavior is a part, and the setting where they take place" (p. 337). Clearly a context is not a neutral setting; in fact, it is not even really a place. Rather, contexts are cultural phenomena, organized in terms of cultural systems of meaning, according to the beliefs, tools, traditions, and practices of cultural groups (Cole and Cole 1993). None of us can experience the world and understand it directly. We meet the world in contexts, selected and organized for us by those who went before and where our groups' cultural tools (e.g., mediating systems like language) are available and can be put to use. Contexts for learning are cultural settings. Although they vary from society to society and even from generation to generation, they are not randomly arranged. Rather, they reflect the history and culture of the group that has organized them. The physical walls of classrooms certainly encompass many contexts. However, if a classroom is not organized so that it can mediate a student's meeting with the world, then it is not a context for that student's learning.

In sum, this is the most intriguing aspect of classrooms: They may or may not be contexts where children can enter into interactions that can trigger and foster development and learning. Although there may be language in use and ongoing interaction, a classroom may not be a context where a child can learn. From observations of classrooms, it is possible to abstract a great deal of knowledge about the cultural beliefs that organize them. Through observation and analysis, it is also possible to distinguish between arrangements of people and activities that are truly contexts for learning and those that are not. As noted above, I contend that deaf children lack access to the most fundamental cultural tools for learning: a historically developed natural language and opportunities to interact with members of that language's community of users in learning contexts organized for them. The current popularity of integrated education, where deaf children are placed (with "appropriate" support) into classrooms designed for hearing speakers of English provides a variety of settings where theoretical ideas about language, interaction, and context can be explored and where contexts for learning can be distinguished from placements in the least restrictive environment. This was the goal of my study of Aspen Elementary School and its program for deaf and hard of hearing students.

Chapter 2

Aspen School:

The Players, the Plan, the Analysis

Aspen Elementary School is a regular public elementary school (K–5) in the United States. It is located in an unincorporated urban area, that is, an area with a relatively dense population that is not within the limits of any city. This community of approximately fifty thousand has a low tax base and no industry and is bounded by a medium-sized city, a large military complex, a small city, and several unincorporated areas, some of them rural. The socioeconomic status of the six thousand students in the school district ranged from low to moderate income. Aspen School was located in a low-income area of the district, and of the school's 359 students, almost half qualified for the free or reduced-price lunch program. Many of the students had at least one parent on active military duty, and several of the deaf students resided with their families in housing on a military base. The school had two general education classrooms each for kindergarten, first, and third through fifth grade. During the study, the second grade population was large, and three classes were formed. With one exception, classes for hearing children had approximately thirty-five students.

Aspen School also housed the district's elementary "deaf and hard of hearing" program that offered classes for preschool through fifth-grade students who were identified as needing some level of supplementary educational support because of hearing impairment or deafness. Through a contracting agreement, deaf and hard of hearing students from several neighboring rural school districts were also enrolled in Aspen School's deaf and hard of hearing program. In fact, during the study year, only two students in the class I studied were from Aspen School's district. The others all rode to school in special buses, vans, or cars provided by their home districts. All of these students had lengthy rides from their homes to school, none traveling for less than an hour each way. The program served between thirty and thirty-five students distributed over four self-contained classrooms: a preschool, a kindergarten, a primary class (approximately grades one, two, and three), and an intermediate class (grades four and five). In addition to self-contained classes, there was also a school policy that all deaf and hard of hearing students be mainstreamed for at least part of each day unless or until a compelling reason arose to prevent it.

TEACHERS AND STUDENTS

The study was conducted in two classrooms: the self-contained classroom for the primary-level deaf students and the regular second-grade classroom where the deaf second graders went each afternoon for their mainstreaming periods. In the self-contained classroom, I observed two teachers of the deaf, Ms. Roberts and Ms. Adams; one instructional assistant/sign language interpreter, Mrs. Hart; and the three boys, Robbie, Tom, and Paul. (The primary class as a whole included ten other second- and third-grade hearing impaired students and two other instructional assistants.) In the mainstreaming classroom I observed one second-grade teacher, Mrs. Rogers, and around twenty hearing second-grade students. This class was smaller than other classes at the school. During the first weeks of the school year, two exceedingly large second-grade classes had been divided into three, and an additional teacher was hired. Although Mrs. Rogers had relatively few students during the morning, five deaf and hard of hearing students joined her class in the afternoons. Her class of hearing students was small to compensate for the added duties that came with her status as a mainstreaming teacher.

For several reasons, I focused on only three deaf children—Tom, Paul, and Robbie. Although there were thirteen children in the self-contained classroom, their complicated daily and weekly schedules were split between several classrooms and between nine different adults, including teachers, instructional assistants, interpreters, speech therapists, "specialist teachers," and others. In order to do the detailed observations I had planned, I felt it necessary to narrow the field. The three boys were the only profoundly deaf second graders that year, and none had disabilities or behavior problems that drastically interfered with their school life. Having known each other for several years, they also formed a social group in their class. Two of them, Tom and Robbie, had been friends and classmates for five years—since preschool. Finally, the fact that Mrs.

Hart, the interpreter who worked with them, was a native signer from a deaf extended family, offered a unique opportunity to observe the use of ASL in a public school program.[1]

Since there were no profoundly deaf girls in that age group during the study year, this is a study of deaf *boys* rather than deaf *children*. Gender plays a role in children's social life, their interactions with others, and their language and literacy activities in school at that age (Dyson 1989, 1994). In fact, both Ms. Adams and Ms. Roberts voiced this concern about the study. The fact is, however, that there are overall more deaf boys than deaf girls (Schein 1996). In a field study like this, the field provides the participants.

ADULTS AND CHILDREN

Of the two teachers of the deaf, Ms. Roberts was the more experienced, with a twelve-year career in deaf education. Before she returned to graduate school to earn a master's degree in deaf education, she had taught hearing elementary school students for three years. Ms. Adams was in her second year of teaching. She had attended and graduated from the same university master's degree program in deaf education that Ms. Roberts had attended more than a decade earlier.

Although she was an experienced elementary teacher and had taught other grades, Mrs. Rogers, the mainstreaming teacher, was in her second year of teaching second grade. She had also served as a school librarian. The study was conducted during her second year as the second-grade mainstreaming teacher.

Mrs. Hart, an instructional assistant, worked with the second graders

1. Five second-grade students were in the primary self-contained class during the study year. Tom, Paul, and Robbie had two hard of hearing classmates—a girl, Drew, and a boy, Lawrence—who did not sign well when the study began.

Lawrence began to develop signing competence during the study year. This facilitated his social life among the second-grade deaf boys, and since he was included as a friend during peer activities, he was sometimes present during observations. Drew rejected both signing and her male classmates during the school year and was rarely included in the boys' social life. In addition, she was almost completely mainstreamed in the regular second-grade. She was included in few observations; nevertheless, she and the fact that she wore hearing aids but did not sign were topics of the boys' conversation.

and went with them to the second-grade mainstreaming classroom. (For consistency and ease of scheduling, each grade level group of deaf and hard of hearing students worked with one instructional assistant/interpreter exclusively.) Mrs. Hart had worked at Aspen School for three years and had previously taught independent living skills to developmentally disabled adults.

Both Ms. Roberts and Ms. Adams are hearing native speakers of English without deaf family members. Each of them had taken American Sign Language and sign language interpreting courses. Native signers who viewed a videotape of the classroom commented that, although it was clear that they were hearing signers, they used ASL. (Native signers' intuitive judgments about the classroom are reported in more detail in Ramsey [1993].)

In contrast, Mrs. Hart has many deaf family members. An audiologist would diagnose her as a patient with a congenital, severe to profound, sensorineural hearing loss who could benefit from amplification in both ears. For her part, Mrs. Hart considered herself a deaf person who is only "a little bit hard of hearing" from a deaf point of view (Padden and Humphries 1989). That is, she can hear a little bit when using her hearing aids, and she can speak to hearing people, but her native and primary language is ASL. Only a "little bit" different from other Deaf people, she feels closer to and more comfortable in the deaf world than in the hearing world.

Tom and Paul both have profound, bilateral sensorineural hearing losses, with no response to speech reception and speech discrimination tests. Each boy had meningitis at around the age of twelve months, which reportedly caused their deafness. According to his records, Tom experienced an "adequate gain" in his hearing when his hearing aids were working and when he wore them. Tom, who turned eight during the study, lost his right hearing aid that year. Paul reportedly experienced an "excellent gain" in his hearing when his hearing aids were working and when he wore them. He did not like his right hearing aid and regularly complained that it was "too noisy." Indeed, results of another audiological test during the study—when Paul was nine—suggested that the right aid was of limited benefit.

Robbie, who turned eight during the study, has a profound sensorineural hearing loss in his left ear and a severe sensorineural hearing loss in his right ear, with no response to speech reception and speech discrimination tests. His audiological report noted that he experienced an "adequate gain" in his hearing when his hearing aids were working and when he wore them. Robbie was born deaf, although the exact cause of his deafness was unknown.

Tom, an only child with hearing, English-speaking parents, entered the preschool deaf and hard of hearing program at Aspen School when he was three years old. Robbie and his parents participated in a university-based parent-infant program when he was a baby, and like Tom, he entered the Aspen School preschool program at the age of three. (He and Tom entered that program the same year.) Paul did not receive schooling of any kind until he entered the Aspen School program at the age of five.

Although the boys' families were not proficient signers, none of them opposed signing. Tom's mother signed and his father signed "some." He had, however, repeatedly stated to the two teachers his belief that it was important to use ASL with Tom "because he'll be part of the Deaf community when he grows up." Paul's parents spoke English at home, although only his father was a native speaker. According to the teachers, before Paul started school, he had been "sitting around" with virtually no communication since infancy. Paul's father began "trying" to sign with him when he was four years old. His mother and the other members of the household (his aunt, a family friend, and her child, whom Paul called his "brother") did not sign. Robbie was the middle child in a hearing English-speaking family, with an older and a younger brother. According to the teachers, his mother signed and his father "tried," and Robbie reported with pride that his twelve-year-old brother was also learning to sign and fingerspell.

CLASSROOM OBSERVATIONS AND ACTIVITIES

This book grounds sociolinguistic data on classroom contexts and language use in the world of an elementary school mainstreaming program for deaf children. The data were generated through participant observation in the self-contained and mainstreaming classrooms as well as through formal and informal interviews with the primary participants. Two video cameras recorded routine, naturally occurring events in the classrooms. The videotapes made it possible to capture the language the deaf children used at school and the functions it served. In addition I wrote narrative fieldnotes, collected copies of student writing and other schoolwork, and copies of the stories the children read. These varied sources of data made it possible to describe the social and linguistic contexts created for, and by, the deaf children during the school day.

During my first visit to the self-contained classroom, Ms. Roberts introduced me to the students as a student, explaining that I was interested in deaf children and what they did at school. I answered the students' questions and asked for their assent to participate. (This included their puzzled queries about what grade I was in, and their horrified questions about whether "grade twenty-three" was required.) All of the children agreed to allow me to visit, observe them, and videotape them. The teachers' and parents' written consents were also obtained at this time.

During the first two weeks of visits I did not use video equipment but observed classroom life and the organization of the school day instead. I discovered that peer interaction was permitted in the self-contained class, and that Ms. Roberts, Ms. Adams, and Mrs. Hart participated in a great deal of conversation with the students. Easing myself into the role of active participant observer, I made no effort to disguise my intentions or to avoid participation in classroom activities. If students drew me in or teachers needed assistance, I participated, although I always referred discipline to the other adults. The deaf students, who observed me as much as I observed them, assigned me the ambiguous status they reserved for hearing signers (people who can both talk and sign). They also treated me as a dependable and cooperative source of information and conversation. After I introduced the video cameras (with which the children were much more familiar than the teachers), an argument arose among the students that lasted almost the entire year. Some claimed that I was merely "curious," whereas others held that I was "snoopy." This issue, which lurks within all fieldwork, was never resolved.

I visited Aspen School sixty-eight times during the school year and spent approximately 250 hours in the self-contained and mainstreaming classrooms and in other school settings (e.g., recess, lunch periods, and field trips). The study yielded approximately 110 hours of videotapes of the children with both adult and peer interlocutors.

The adults in the study were able to ignore the equipment when they were busy with their work but expressed some embarrassment and discomfort with it when they had time to reflect on the constant presence of cameras. All of the children were familiar with video cameras and generally paid no attention to them. Nevertheless, they were curious about what I was taping and sometimes fooled around or made faces on camera.

Twice during the study year, I showed the children tapes of themselves, including a tape that the teachers and I made of the students as a pilot test of the video equipment near the beginning of the year. My last classroom visit was devoted to viewing tapes selected from each month of the school year, so that the students could see how much they had changed and remember some of their activities in Ms. Roberts's and Ms. Adams's room.

I taped classroom activities and interaction as they occurred naturally. The children and teachers were not asked to move from their chosen seats or to move furniture during videotaping. No participants were asked to avoid walking in front of the cameras. Only participants who presented signed consent forms were videotaped. If I arrived at the school and found a substitute teacher or interpreter, no videotaped observations were made that day, although I often stayed to observe the children and to help out in the classroom. In addition, I never videotaped activities when I was not present, so that I was participating and observing during each day of data collection, making notes to fill out the videotapes.

For the first month of the study (mid-September to mid-October), I spent the entire school day at the school and observed all thirteen deaf second- and third-graders during group lesson times, the only time of day the whole class was together. In addition, I observed small group activities when the students sat in grade-level groups at different tables. The teachers and instructional assistants worked with the students in groups ranging in size from one student (a second-grade reading "group") to seven or eight (for example, a third-grade spelling lesson). Most of the instruction was carried out in small groups, and my preliminary observations included spelling instruction, silent reading time, and journal writing and other writing activities as well as "calendar-time"[2] and periods of free time that the children earned with good behavior.

2. Calendar time was Ms. Roberts's term for the first event of the school day, when children were welcomed to school and oriented to the activities and responsibilities for the day. During this period they discussed the weather, current events, and the calendar: days of the week, months and seasons of the year, and holidays. Calendar time in the self-contained classroom was a commonplace elementary school ritual that generally had nothing to do with deafness and everything to do with the routines of American elementary school life. In addition, to foster a sense of belonging to a world of deaf children and adults outside the school, the adults arranged regular visits from deaf people. So that their group of thirty-five students

Early observations also included a lesson referred to as "language." These lessons were conducted in a mix of ASL, sign-supported speech, speech, and writing and were built around topics like feelings, school rules, or healthy foods. To teach content and to give the students opportunities to take extended turns communicating with the group, the teachers used the period to introduce vocabulary in both printed English and in signs and fingerspelling. If a topic emerged that the students found interesting, the teachers would allow the conversation to shift and, as Ms. Roberts expressed it, "just let them go," that is, let the students pursue the topics that arose in the group.

Early in the school year I also met with two mainstreaming teachers (one regular second-grade teacher and one regular third-grade teacher) to explain the project and arrange for an exploratory visit to their classrooms when the deaf students and interpreters were there. Visits to each class during mainstreaming periods lasted from one to two hours, during which I observed a math lesson and a science lesson in the second grade mainstreaming classroom and a math lesson in the third grade mainstreaming classroom. Each teacher and each interpreter was willing to accommodate my presence in the classroom, and neither teacher objected to video equipment. At this time, I also obtained the consent of the hearing students (and their parents) in the mainstreaming classes.

In mid-October I began videotaping recurring activities in both the self-contained and mainstreaming classrooms. The events of interest in the self-contained classroom were calendar time and language period, spelling lessons, journal writing, book-reading/sharing lessons, and free time. In addition, I videotaped the regular Friday morning visits of local Deaf people. In the mainstreaming classroom, where Mrs. Hart interpreted, I observed math, science, social studies, and art. The routine interactions of each deaf student with the hearing students at his table were videotaped. In addition, samples of interpreted instruction were videotaped, including both Mrs. Rogers' spoken English and Mrs. Hart's sign language interpretation. I also visited and observed lunchtime and recesses although these two events were not videotaped.

In March I stopped observing in the mainstreaming classroom and observed and videotaped Tom, Robbie, and Paul only when they were

---

could meet other deaf children, they occasionally organized field trips to the state residential school or to an interpreted play attended by deaf children from many mainstreaming programs in the region.

writing and reading in the self-contained classroom. The recurring activities of interest were "journal time" (which included both writing and drawing and during which conversation was allowed), reading lessons (which Tom and Paul usually had together with Ms. Roberts, while Robbie read alone with Ms. Adams), and "silent reading," an event that was generally unsupervised and provided many opportunities for conversation among the boys.

In addition to the recurring literacy activities, another event—a lengthy, integrated language arts unit—took place during spring of the school year. Ms. Roberts was known among the deaf students for organizing multimedia units in her classroom, and during the study year the topic was Guatemala, where she had lived and traveled. She began by showing slides of her travels in Central America, putting up maps and photographs, and bringing books and *National Geographic* magazines to share with the children. Under her guidance, the entire second- and third-grade self-contained class discussed Guatemala, its prehistory, history, culture, and languages. The unit spanned several weeks. Through class discussions, many new ideas were generated, and the students drew pictures and wrote reports about aspects of Guatemala that they found interesting. At the end of the unit, the students' reports and pictures were compiled into a booklet, and each student received a copy. Finally, toward the end of the unit, the students—some of them dressed in Guatemalan clothing provided by Ms. Roberts—invited the kindergarten deaf and hard of hearing class to their room, and the students read their reports to the younger children.

Throughout the year I interviewed Mrs. Hart, Ms. Roberts, Ms. Adams, and Mrs. Rogers individually and at length about mainstreaming. In addition, I spoke with Mrs. Hart about deafness in general and about her own experiences in a deaf family, including raising her deaf children. Once I interviewed Ms. Roberts and Ms. Adams together about their classroom and the students, then each individually twice about her training and her beliefs about deaf education and classroom language. Interviews were documented with audiotape and/or with handwritten notes and transcribed or fleshed out later. All the adults spoke English during their interviews, although Mrs. Hart shifted between spoken English and ASL.

In May I interviewed—in ASL—the three boys about school, reading and writing, friends, hearing and Deaf people, and signing and speech training. Interview topics were pilot tested with several third-grade deaf students before the three second-graders were interviewed. Each interview was videotaped and transcribed in English glosses.

VIDEOTAPES, CONVERSATIONS, JOURNALS, AND READING

For purposes of analysis, I envisioned the physical site of Aspen School as existing among and creating several kinds of school contexts, each of which influenced face-to-face language use for the deaf students and their opportunities for learning and development. The entire school was deeply embedded in the familiar political context of "special education" in the United States. In turn, this broad set of beliefs influenced the structure of the two classrooms where Tom, Robbie, and Paul had their schooling— the mainstreaming classroom and the self-contained classroom—the settings through which the deaf students maneuvered as students, as language users, and as literacy learners.

The mainstreaming program at Aspen School offered a particular instance of the contemporary special education practice of integration in the United States. My analysis is based on data collected during observations in mainstreaming settings and from interviews with teachers, instructional assistants, the interpreter, and the deaf students. Finding several consistencies in fieldnotes and interview transcripts, I identified the salient dimensions of mainstreaming at Aspen School. These include the conflicting definitions of deaf children and their needs, the struggle to enact a "least restrictive environment," and the frequent references to the law and to civil rights issues.

Videotapes of the mainstreaming classroom examine interactions between the deaf boys and their hearing peers. Due to the very traditional, teacher-centered instruction in the mainstreaming classroom, the main actors in face-to-face communication in these settings were other students: the deaf students' hearing classmates. Mrs. Rogers rarely interacted one-on-one with her students. Accordingly, peer conversations constituted the units of interest. Close examination of peer interaction also presented an opportunity to examine the processes by which assimilation of deaf and hearing children might take place in the mainstreaming setting, the location upon which administrators and policymakers place high expectations.

I analyzed peer conversations during recurrent classroom events, including art, social studies, and "rainy day recess" periods. Analysis was based on specific sociolinguistic features, the setting and participants, the language used, and the functions for which the language was employed. These features were coded from videotapes. The limited inventory of functions that appeared in deaf-hearing peer interactions was compared to a longer list of possible functions of language (Dyson 1989); from this contrast, I developed the notion of "caretaker" functions of language (discussed in chapter 5).

In contrast to the mainstreaming classroom, the self-contained classroom was organized to promote a great deal of interaction and communication. All participants—children and adults—were involved in conversation much of the time. This analysis focuses on interaction among the three students, Tom, Robbie, and Paul, and the three adults (Mrs. Hart, who acted as an important source of ASL, and Ms. Adams and Ms. Roberts, who were very proficient signers, although neither was a native signer).

I analyzed a variety of recurrent activities in the self-contained classroom, including language study, journal writing, silent reading, and story-reading/book-sharing period.[3] These events provided consistent manifestations of the interactional rules of the self-contained classroom as well as many examples of the ways the children used language to keep their own ideas and objectives at the forefront in their attempts to organize classroom activities and interactions for their own purposes.

All conversations within these events were coded for participants, language used, and functions of language employed, and some sections were transcribed. Conversations were identified by boundaries, that is, initiations (conventional signed initiations like HEY, touching, tapping the table, eye contact) and terminations (generally an interlocutor looking away or making a more explicit utterance, such as "I'm ignoring you"). As with analysis of face-to-face language in the mainstreaming setting, this analysis focused on the participants, the forms of language used, and the functions for which it was employed. Included in the analysis of classroom language in the self-contained classroom were analyses of the deaf students' conversations, drawing, and writing during journal time. In theoretical terms, I regarded the journal writing activity as a particularly intriguing instance of "the-individual-acting-with-mediational-means" (Wertsch 1989).

3. I am grateful to Susan Sterne for assistance with coding and analysis of these events.

Journal writing also illustrated the functions of talk that surround early writing. Dyson (1991) describes hearing children's uses for spoken language as they move along the developmental path toward writing. Tom, Robbie, and Paul used ASL for similar purposes, including signing to adults and to themselves. Accordingly, I analyzed their reliance on the language with which they are more familiar, ASL, as they tried to produce English.

The goal of analysis was to illustrate the contrasts in opportunities for language use in a variety of settings in a public elementary school mainstreaming program. All analyses were qualitative, that is, coding categories emerged from the data during repeated viewings of videotapes, bolstered with data from field notes and teacher and student interviews. The research was designed to reveal the different levels that determine deaf children's opportunities to learn and use language at school, based on the theoretical assumption that deaf children's use of language at school is a crucial contributor to their school achievement, particularly their progress toward literacy.

NATIVE SIGNER JUDGMENTS

To elicit the intuitions of native signers about the adult and child signing in this classroom, traditional linguistic fieldwork methods were followed. Following established convention, a *native signer* is defined as a deaf person with deaf parents whose first language was ASL, or a deaf person with hearing parents who attended residential school from the age of six or earlier (Woodward 1973). Three native signers agreed to serve as linguistic consultants. Two have deaf parents and siblings, and one has hearing parents and grew up in a residential school from the age of six. The third consultant was also the mother of a deaf school-age child. All were recommended by other members of the Deaf community, and all three were identified as deaf native signers.

All three consultants lived within two hundred miles of the study site; none, however, recognized any of the children or adults on the videotapes. Linguistic judgments were gathered during visits to the home or office of each deaf signer. Each session of viewing and discussion lasted approximately one and one-half hours. The consultants knew they would see and comment on a tape of a classroom with three teachers, three deaf students, and two hard of hearing students. The type of school program (residential or public school mainstreaming program) was not identified nor was there any indication as to whether the teachers were deaf or hearing; no details were divulged about the students. Each consultant viewed three sample events (a language lesson, a reading-writing activity, and a book-sharing event). Afterward, they reported what kinds of signing they felt they had seen and expressed many opinions about the state of education for deaf children today. Independently, each consultant characterized the children as ASL signers, Mrs. Hart as a deaf person who probably had deaf parents, and the teachers as hearing people who were late learners of ASL but who were trying to use it.

This book differs from traditional reports about deaf education. It is not a study that evaluates or assesses the achievement of individual deaf children. It is not a study of educational outcomes. Rather it is a descriptive study of everyday life in a public elementary school program for deaf students and hard of hearing students. An important goal of this book is to provide a glimpse into a typical school program for deaf students, to put into human terms the consequences of placement decisions. The seemingly rational choices that are made from the range of placement options must be informed decisions. However, information on the everyday school lives of elementary deaf students in public schools is often the precise thing that is missing when the options are reviewed.

Tom, Robbie, and Paul were like the majority of deaf elementary students. They had hearing parents, attended a local public school, and were struggling to develop basic literacy skills. They were unable to read well enough to understand their mainstreaming textbooks, still on grade level at math computation and memory for "math facts," but poor at comprehending and carrying out story problems. In the self-contained classroom, they did well on spelling tests. Their writing skills were variable, but each had some knowledge of English rules and the conventions of writing. The program described here was neither a "bad" nor a "good" program. It was a typical program, staffed with teachers with a range of expertise, who maintained distinct stances toward their jobs but who felt they knew what was best for the deaf students. At school, as in most contexts, this was not necessarily easy to determine.

Chapter 3

Placements and Contexts: What Is a Public

School Deaf and Hard of Hearing Program?

Over time, I noticed an intriguing contrast in the ways the deaf children were perceived by school personnel. The special education administrators, the principal, and most of the general education staff viewed the deaf students very differently from the way they were regarded by the teachers and staff of the deaf and hard of hearing program. Deeply concerned about their obligation to place the deaf children appropriately, the former group spoke of following legislative guidelines and identifying "least restrictive environments." On the other hand, Ms. Roberts, Ms. Adams, and Mrs. Hart rarely discussed these topics. Their most common consideration was the educational needs of deaf children in general. The deaf and hard of hearing program staff were most involved with how to structure their classroom so that Tom, Robbie, and Paul and their classmates could develop the basic skills needed to proceed successfully through elementary, middle, and high schools. The distinction between educational placements and contexts for learning for deaf students does not exist in a vacuum and was not unique to Aspen School. On the contrary, concerns about school placement are among the most durable in deaf education (e.g., Commission 1988), and disputes about where deaf students' schooling should properly take place have a long history (e.g., Moores 1996; Lane et al. 1996).

The first schools for deaf students in the United States were residential schools in Hartford, Connecticut (1817), New York (1818), and Philadelphia (1820). As time passed, similar special schools, both state supported and private, were founded in other states, and by 1860 there were more than twenty schools for deaf students in the country. By the mid-twentieth century each state had at least one school, and until the 1960s the majority of deaf students attended a school for deaf students, either a residential school or a special day school. After World War II, the trend in the

United States toward offering education for deaf children in local schools rather than in residential schools (Moores 1996; Commission 1988) culminated in a rapid increase in local public school deaf education programs beginning in the 1970s. Two events contributed to this trend. First, the 1963–1965 rubella epidemic engendered a large group of deaf children who needed schooling. Because existing programs could not absorb this large population of students, new local programs were created. Second, PL 94-142 (now termed the Individuals with Disabilities Education Act or IDEA) was enacted in 1975. This law and its accompanying regulations and guidelines codified the notion of educating students with disabilities in the least restrictive environment (or LRE). Although not explicitly stated in the text, the law was widely interpreted as favoring educating children with disabilities in local public schools.

PL 94-142 and IDEA are built upon an important American ideal: that society is obligated to provide equal educational opportunity for Americans with disabilities, a group that has been shamefully underserved by educational institutions in the past. Pointing out the weaknesses in the implementation of this ideal is not a rejection of the ideal itself. However, in critical ways, the ideas suggested by or codified in these laws have overlooked the social obligation of schools to actually educate students with disabilities once they are invited into the school building. In particular, the belief that integration with able-bodied peers is the preferred vehicle for ensuring educational opportunity has motivated many of the policy changes that grew out of PL 94-142. In the process, the specific developmental and educational needs of young deaf Americans have been underestimated.

The LRE has been the most confusing and controversial legacy of PL 94-142/IDEA. Given the wide range of abilities, learning preferences, and objectives found in this large, highly diverse group, defining the "appropriate" and the "least restrictive" settings for teaching and learning among disabled students is not a simple task. In addition, conflicting notions of appropriateness and restriction easily arise because several people participate in educational decisions made on behalf of a student with disabilities. The outcome has often been that LRE is taken at its most literal meaning to indicate a setting where no visible barriers are apparent. Regular settings with architectural, technological, or human accommodations that seem to eliminate obstacles and make it possible for able-bodied and disabled students to be integrated are favored. Despite the fact that the law itself does not explicitly advocate "mainstreaming" or even integration, some people (beginning with Large 1980) have suggested that a philosophical stance against segregation underlies the law and its implementation. Since the LRE requirement is most often taken as a statement about physical placement rather than as an assertion about learning and teaching, decision makers may overlook or underestimate the many specific needs of students with different disabilities. The consequence for deaf students has been a narrow definition of their educational needs, which often rests on the assumption that deaf children need hearing children as models of appropriate behavior and as models of standard language and conventional communication. Some Aspen School staff held this belief despite the fact that the hearing students did not sign, the deaf students did not speak, and the two groups really had no common meeting ground.

It may be very difficult to change a deaf student's placement from an integrated to a self-contained classroom, even if this will promote the student's learning. Such a circumstance arose at Aspen School during my research. One of the deaf third-grade students, placed in a regular third-grade class for math, completed the math book on his own in March, well before the end of the school year. Although it was clear that he possessed superior math abilities, the regular teacher declined to provide more advanced materials. As a solution to the child's need for challenging math lessons to continue his rapid progress, Ms. Roberts (with the parents' permission) proposed to the district that she provide math instruction in the self-contained classroom. The district did not consider this a suitable solution since it entailed a "demotion" from the perceived least restrictive environment to a more restrictive setting. The child's accelerated math achievement was not considered a critical factor in this decision. This is but one example of the ideological bind that LRE has created among educators. Ironically, the people who need to be convinced that a change in placement is in order are often regular classroom teachers and school district administrators, who generally have little preparation for understanding the educational consequences of deafness and the needs of deaf children. This situation, coupled with the funding mechanisms of public education, covertly promotes education in regular classroom settings, especially for elementary level students. Mainstreaming, and now "full inclusion," are both organizational mechanisms for creating integrated settings.

Mainstreaming is the popular term that has described integrated educational placements for deaf children. In "continuum" or "cascade" models of services for students with disabilities (Gearhart, Mullen, and Gearhart 1993), integrated or mainstream settings are preferred on the assumption that they constitute the least restrictive placement option. Separate classes and special schools are among the least preferred placement options under this model. In fact, Gearhart et al. (1993) claim that segregated settings are "rarely required but must be provided when they are the most appropriate placement" (p. 42). Although used as a general replacement term for mainstreaming, the term *full inclusion* actually indicates a distinct—and radical—view of school restructuring (Ramsey 1994). Specifically, under the full inclusion model, all students, disabled and able bodied, are placed in regular education classrooms—all day, everyday. Within regular classrooms, students with disabilities receive support from regular education teachers and other specialists as needed in order to achieve the goals that are set for them. Hypothetically, they are not considered visitors to regular classrooms, as mainstreamed students often are, but genuine participants in all of classroom life. Among supporters of this model are educators who believe that the current system of special education is obsolete and unjust and should be completely eliminated (Stainback, Stainback, and Bunch 1989).

Mainstreaming was the term used at Aspen School to describe the deaf students' placement (with interpreters) into classes with hearing children. The newer terms "full inclusion" and "inclusive education" sometimes appear in general usage, and in some parts of the country, for some students with disabilities, implementation of "full inclusion" has eclipsed the practice of mainstreaming. Full inclusion, however, has rarely been applied to deaf students, even in districts that have implemented it for other groups. Mainstreaming is still the most widespread term—as well as the most common integration technique—used in deaf education. It is also the expression used in the Deaf community to describe mixed hearing and deaf classes in public schools. Indeed, some deaf signers refer to public school deaf and hard of hearing programs as mainstreaming programs even if the deaf and hearing students do not have classes together. Yet the term itself masks a very complicated pattern of enrollment among deaf and hard of hearing students in the United States.

The Aspen School mainstreaming teachers had very limited preparation for working with deaf and hard of hearing students. This situation is not uncommon. Although in some schools mainstreaming and special education teachers work more closely together, training and support vary widely, from the very close relationships among teachers reported in Banks (1994) to the great distance reported by others. A high school English teacher reported that an orally schooled deaf student (with no interpreter) was placed in her class. The decision was made to withhold the details of this nonsigning student's disability on the grounds that informing the teacher would betray a confidence and invade the deaf student's privacy. The student struggled with the course content and the class assignments. Mystified by the situation, the teacher was unable to provide appropriate assistance and was not enlightened until well into the term when the school principal reluctantly revealed the facts (Largent, personal communication).

Indeed, administrative support, especially the active interest of the school principal, is a critical factor according to both Higgins (1990) and Banks (1994). In particular, the principal's level of involvement and commitment often determines whether the mainstreaming program and the students with disabilities are an integral part of the school or constitute a marginal activity that takes place in a parallel world within the same building. Higgins suggests that the principal's commitment can be assessed through routine matters such as the setting of mainstreaming schedules as well as extraordinary actions such as the principal's learning to sign.

Despite administrative approaches to mainstreaming, general education teachers are the frontline personnel when students with distinctive educational needs appear in their classes. Scruggs and Mastropieri (1996) conducted a metanalysis of survey data gathered from general and special education teachers between 1958 and 1995. They report that most general and special education teachers feel that the former lack sufficient training and expertise to receive students with disabilities into their classes. Very few general education teachers felt qualified to address— without supportive assistance—the special needs of mainstreamed children, although most agreed that in-service training would be helpful and that they could acquire techniques to help them foster achievement in students with mild disabilities. The report of the Commission on Education of the Deaf (1988) also suggests that mainstreaming teachers need additional training in order to promote the learning of deaf and hard of hearing students.

Overall, the teachers in the Scruggs and Mastropieri metanalysis (1996) felt they had insufficient time for mainstreaming. Although most claimed to need at least one additional hour of planning time per day in order to prepare for students with disabilities, this time was rarely available to them; most of the respondents had less than thirty minutes of additional planning time per day. In addition, most teachers felt that they did not have enough resources to support mainstreaming programs. Although some felt that material resources were sufficient, most stated that they did not have adequate personnel support. The attitudes that Scruggs and Mastropieri report do not co-vary with either geographical region or year of publication. That is, despite the changes in policy since the mid-'70s, the attitudes and the preparation of general education teachers do not appear to have changed.

CONTEMPORARY PATTERNS OF PLACEMENT FOR DEAF STUDENTS

Demographic studies provide evidence that, in reality, mainstreaming is not a straightforward matter of physically integrating all students with hearing impairments into classes with hearing students. Placement decisions are influenced by the students' ages, ethnicities, and degrees of hearing loss. Simple counts of deaf students in various settings mask a much more interesting demographic situation. The majority of deaf students, approximately 70 percent, now attend local public schools (Schildroth and Hotto 1995), a finding that may mean that deaf and hearing students are well integrated in America's classrooms. However, the details of local school programs and the placement decisions that occur there present a different picture. Characteristics of individual deaf students influence the placement decisions made on their behalf. Deaf students' everyday school lives in local public school programs vary widely across the school-age population.

It is critical to bear in mind that deafness is a low-incidence condition. The school-age contingent of deaf and hard of hearing students in the United States is approximately fifty thousand (Schildroth 1988). Schildroth reports that the number of local public schools offering deaf education programs almost doubled between 1977–78 and 1985–86. One result is that 52 percent of the schools that reported having a deaf and hard of hearing program served only one "hearing impaired" student. An additional 16 percent of the school programs reported serving only two students. Although this finding specifies neither the severity of the students' hearing losses nor the extent of their integration with hearing children, it suggests that a portion of the deaf and hard of hearing school-age population either does not know any other deaf children or has contact with only one other deaf or hard of hearing child. These enrollment patterns have serious implications for deaf students in the context of the developmental theory outlined earlier, which assumes that social life and interaction in school contexts promote learning. Aspen School drew several such children, including Robbie and Tom, who would have been the only deaf or hard of hearing student in their home districts if they had remained there. The contracting arrangement between Aspen School and these districts guaranteed a fairly large group in their deaf and hard of hearing program. Robbie, Tom, and Paul were fortunate to be part of a relatively large elementary-aged cohort: thirty-five students in grades K–5. There were thirteen children between the ages of seven and ten.

The three boys attended a regular second-grade class for one and a half to two hours a day for a variety of activities, including math, social studies, science, art, PE, music, library, and recess. Social studies and science alternated, and each was offered every other day. Library period occurred once a week, and music and PE were offered for alternating three-week periods. This means that the deaf children participated in a range of mainstreaming lessons for about nine or ten hours a week, but not all of the lessons occurred on the same day. How does their pattern of mainstreaming compare to those identified for their demographic peers, other eight- and nine-year-olds in the larger national cohort of deaf and hard of hearing students?

Elementary-age deaf students are more likely than secondary-level students to be in local public school programs, although most of them are not placed in integrated classes. Holt (1995) reports that age is significantly related to placement. In demographic, communication mode, and achievement data collected in 1990, the majority (64 percent) of elementary level students (ages 8 to 12) attended local public schools. However, only about one-third of them were integrated for six or more hours per week, barely an hour a day. (In contrast, the majority of twelve- to seventeen-year-olds attend special schools for the deaf.) The 1992–1993

Annual Survey of Deaf and Hard of Hearing Children and Youth (CADS 1992–1993) is consistent with Holt's findings, reporting that more than half of the children like Tom, Robbie, and Paul (eight- and nine-year-olds with severe-profound hearing losses) attended local school programs. These children were integrated with hearing students but for fewer than fifteen hours per week. This would account for up to half of their time at school. Very few of the eight- and nine-year-olds in this group (only about 14 percent) were integrated for more than fifteen hours per week. Although most deaf students like the Aspen School children attend local public schools, these numbers suggest that they attend mainstreamed classes less than half of the time. The assumption is that the rest of the time they are in self-contained classes with specially trained teachers of the deaf, that is, in nonintegrated settings.

Studies of national patterns of school placement indicate other complications of placement decisions for deaf students. Two static characteristics—degree of hearing loss and ethnic group identity—influence mainstreaming placement as well. In all age groups, students with profound hearing losses, like Tom and Paul, are the most likely to receive no academic integration (CADS 1992–1993). In contrast, Holt (1995) reports that among the 1990 deaf and hard of hearing student population, more than half of students with less-than-severe losses were integrated six or more hours a week. These students were also the most likely to use speech as their primary mode of communication, and most attended mainstreaming classes without interpreters. Ethnic group membership is also associated with likelihood of mainstreaming placement. Holt (1995) reports that among all white deaf and hard of hearing students, 58 percent were mainstreamed for more than six hours per week. In contrast, only 30 percent of all deaf and hard of hearing students from minority groups were placed in mainstreaming settings for more than six hours a week. Among white severely to profoundly deaf students (the least likely to be placed in mainstreaming settings for academics), 20 percent are mainstreamed fifteen or more hours per week. In contrast, students who are severely to profoundly deaf and from another ethnic group (African American, Hispanic, Native American, and Asian/Pacific) are even less likely to be placed in mainstreaming settings. Around 10 percent of severely to profoundly deaf nonwhite students from other groups were placed in integrated settings for more than fifteen hours a week (CADS 1992–1993). Recent demographic research (Padden and Tractenberg 1996) suggests that the majority of students who have deaf parents (a small proportion of the total deaf and hard of hearing school population) enroll at residential schools for the deaf. Accordingly, this group, the majority of which are white, are much less likely to attend public school programs, hence, very unlikely to be placed in mainstreamed settings.

To summarize, the more severe a student's hearing loss, the less likely that student will be mainstreamed. The less severe a student's loss, the more likely that student will speak rather than sign, and the more likely that student will be mainstreamed. White students with hearing parents are more likely to be mainstreamed, even those with severe to profound hearing losses. Since they are rarely found in public school programs, children with deaf parents are very unlikely to be mainstreamed. In reality this means that public school deaf students rarely have peers who are proficient native signers. These facts help to put into perspective the findings on achievement among mainstreamed students.

Several studies (e.g., Allen 1986; Allen and Osborn 1984; Kluwin and Moores 1985) have found an association between placement in regular classes with hearing students and achievement in deaf and hard of hearing students. These studies, however, do not report student achievement prior to placement in integrated settings. This is critical, since commonly reported criteria for selecting deaf and hard of hearing candidates for mainstreaming, specifically good communication abilities and strong academic skills (e.g., Brill 1978; Moores and Kluwin 1986), are almost identical to the reported positive outcomes of mainstreaming (e.g., higher levels of academic functioning and development of a range of communication abilities, including intelligible English, in order to be understood by hearing peers). Holt (1995) reports a similar finding with intriguing detail. She found that fully mainstreamed students who were white and had less than severe hearing losses and no cognitive handicaps achieved the highest reading comprehension and math computation scores in comparisons of students in fully mainstreamed settings, residential schools, and self-contained classes. In addition, students who were enrolled in special schools (i.e., residential or day schools specifically for deaf students) and had severe or profound losses achieved higher scores than students in local public schools who were in self-contained classes. Again, it is critical to note that identifying an association is not the same as explaining its cause. As Holt cautions, we simply do not know whether students are selected for integrated placements because of their academic achievement or whether placement in integrated settings actually causes improvements in academic achievement. One reason the nature of the association is so poorly understood is that mainstreaming includes widely varying practices in extremely diverse settings. A public school that serves only one deaf student will be very different from one that serves thirty-five. In addition, we know very little about classroom discourse, processes of teaching and learning, and the routine details of everyday life for deaf children in mainstreaming settings. That is, whereas we are well informed about the numbers and the characteristics of students who are placed in mainstreaming settings, we know almost nothing about how these settings function as contexts for learning.

In many ways, Robbie, Tom, and Paul were like other deaf children of their age in the United States. They attended a public school deaf and hard of hearing program, and they were in mainstreamed settings between six and fifteen hours per week. Their family backgrounds also suggest that they would be likely candidates for some mainstreaming. They were all from hearing families and were either white or of mixed white and Asian/Pacific Island heritage. Because of their severe to profound hearing losses they were signers who did not use speech. In some ways, however, they were different from other deaf children in the United States. They had some academic subjects in the mainstream class. Unlike many deaf students, they had a relatively large class, which included other children their age. Their general achievement in the mainstreaming classroom, however, was not remarkable. Second-grade math called for memorization of math facts and for some adding and subtracting, which the boys did well. On other academic tasks they did not perform at grade level. Reading and solving story problems in the math book and reading the science and social studies texts were beyond their skills.

Underlying the demographic characteristics of mainstreamed students and their distribution over American public schools are the everyday practices of mainstreaming in public school programs. Mainstreaming has linguistic and academic implications as well as a serious social and cultural impact on deaf students. Often deaf students' academic needs simply cannot be served in these programs. Most elementary deaf children are in public school programs, yet the general achievement of this population is far below what would be expected for hearing children with normal intelligence (Allen 1986). At a time in their lives when they need sustained periods of high-quality, carefully planned instruction to acquire the most basic school skills, including in many cases their first language, their school days are broken up with "pull out" visits to mainstreaming classes. In these settings there is often no one with whom they can directly communicate. Participation in mainstreaming classes depends upon the fluent deployment of basic skills that deaf children have not mastered. (For example, the Aspen School children were often asked to read independently texts that were beyond their comprehension.) Discourse practices that have evolved among hearing teachers (e.g., writing on the board with one's back to the class while explaining what is being written, asking children to follow a text at their desks as the teacher reads aloud) are workable with hearing children, but exclude deaf children even when an interpreter is present (Winston 1992). Indeed, signed instructional discourse requires a completely different quality of attention and fine-tuned pragmatic skills that are difficult for new signers to acquire even in separate classrooms for deaf children (Ramsey and Padden 1996). The linguistic pressures on signing deaf children are tremendous in mainstreaming settings. Contrary to assumptions (Gearhart et al. 1993), being with hearing, speaking children does not automatically guarantee that deaf children will be forced to develop the communication skills required to interact through speech and speechreading. The condition of childhood deafness is not amenable to this type of force, to good intentions, or to the challenge of interacting with hearing children. In addition, it is very difficult for children simultaneously to acquire their first language and the ability to use it as a tool for school learning, although this is the task that many young deaf students face. For children who sign fluently, mainstreaming settings do not provide signing conversational partners unless hearing students and staff have quality sign language instruction and sufficient time to practice signing with deaf signers. Although hearing children sometimes pick up a few signs or the ability to fingerspell, their signs are often incomprehensible to the deaf children, just as the deaf signers' more fluent signing is incomprehensible to the hearing children.

To return briefly to theory, social settings for learning and teaching are critical to fostering children's development. This is true for deaf and hearing children as well as for American, Nepalese, or Danish children. It is simply not possible for an individual child to develop and learn without access to and membership in groups, both local social groups (like classrooms) and cultural groups with histories and practices. A great deal of evidence indicates that mainstreamed deaf children have difficulty participating in the local social groups of hearing children at school (e.g., Antia 1982; Saur et al. 1986). From a theoretical point of view, this means that deaf children in mainstreaming settings have little or no access to the power of social interaction to make learning possible. Deaf children's cultural participation, our most basic and human necessity, is also problematic in mainstreaming settings. Most public school deaf students have little or no access to other Deaf people and to their living culture (Woodward et al. 1988). Because of language barriers, they also have incomplete or distorted access to the living cultures of hearing and speaking people. This includes both the cultural patterns and heritage of their homes as well as the more general American culture embodied in the everyday lives of hearing people. Although the bare numbers may suggest that we are approaching a world where deaf and hearing people will be well integrated, in fact, this hoped-for goal is far from our reach. The ideals upon which integrated education is founded—the desire to create a world of greater opportunity and justice for coming generations of students with disabilities—is difficult to imagine for deaf students under current circumstances. The implicit social contract of schools, which is a promise to parents of deaf children and to society to teach them at least basic skills, has also proven difficult to accomplish.

The current national picture of mainstreaming for deaf and hard of hearing students suggests that this practice is not haphazardly applied to all deaf students. It would be incorrect to claim that all American deaf children are abandoned or "dumped" in regular classes with hearing children. However, the placement of deaf children in mainstream settings occurs frequently, a fact that influences deaf students' learning and development. From my observations, experience, and research, it appears that mainstreaming is conducted primarily for reasons that have little to do with learning and a great deal to do with idealistic goals of equality of opportunity. As teachers attempt to put the ideals into practice, tension between placements and contexts for learning is genuine and is manifested in both their attitudes and their classroom organization.

Chapter 4

Mainstreaming at Aspen School

At Aspen School, LRE and the goal of providing equal educational opportunity created a great deal of tension among the staff. The general education staff and the deaf and hard of hearing program staff differed in their definitions of *restrictive* and *equal*. Much fuss was made over logistical arrangements of the settings where deaf and hearing children were integrated. Observations of daily life and conversations with teachers at the school clarified the difficulty of putting ideals into practice. For most of the general education staff, decisions about the deaf children were based upon provision of equality. Deaf children were students for whom equality had to be arranged in space and in time. The responsibility for taking advantage of physical access to hearing classes to learn belonged to the deaf students. The difficulty of basing teaching practices upon an abstraction like equality is poignantly clear in the teachers' comments about mainstreaming. In interactions between deaf and hearing peers, some of the consequences of misguided placements are evident.

Despite the fact that *restrictive, equality,* and *access* have various meanings, the staff of Aspen School firmly believed that educational equality could be achieved if deaf children were placed in the LRE. Conversations with the primary grade teachers, specialists, and instructional assistants disclosed the fact that they had varying degrees of knowledge about mainstreaming, depending on their involvement with it. (The school principal, who was in his first year on the job, was unavailable for an interview.) To upgrade their training, several teachers had taken weekend workshops or summer courses that were not about deaf students specifically but provided information on the policies that motivated mainstreaming and suggestions for integrating able-bodied students with those with disabilities. When asked about the presence of deaf children at Aspen School, most of the general education teachers routinely reported that the "entire school" was mainstreamed and accessible, offering the presence of interpreters as evidence. Mrs. Rogers, the second-grade mainstreaming teacher, shared this belief. Others commented on the services provided for deaf students or reported their interest in sign language.

With pride, teachers reported, "We have interpreters and interpreted assemblies. It's so much fun to watch the interpreter!" Not surprisingly, many staff told me that they had always wanted to learn to sign or that they wished they had time to learn.

Some teachers privately expressed dissatisfaction with mainstreaming, and most believed that having deaf students who signed in a class with hearing children added to their workload. General education teachers resented both the interruptions to their schedules that resulted from the visits of the deaf children and interpreter as well as the effort required to work with an interpreter. The Aspen School teachers' perspective is not unique but reflects the attitude of general education teachers, who, on the whole, do not embrace mainstreaming. Scruggs and Mastropieri (1996) synthesize research spanning thirty-seven years (1958–1995), analyzing the responses of over ten thousand teachers to mainstreaming. Although a majority supported integrated education as a concept, fewer were willing actually to have students with disabilities in their own classrooms. It was not uncommon for teachers to hypothetically accept a student with a mild disability as long as the teacher did not have complete responsibility for that student. The more severe the disability, the less acceptable the student. About half the teachers agreed that mainstreaming benefits students with disabilities, but most felt that the practice required significant alterations in classroom organization and that they did not have sufficient time, training, or resources to carry out the modifications. In general, Aspen School teachers had the same realistic view of mainstreaming as well as the same lack of training and time.

Some of the negative feelings were residual, resentment carried over from the past when the former school principal simply assigned deaf children to regular classrooms without informing either teachers of the deaf children or the receiving teachers. Although the teachers of the deaf were displeased with this kind of management, they accepted it as simply an extension of the widespread situation facing all teachers of the deaf in small mainstreaming programs: They are most often supervised by a principal who has no special expertise in deaf education, does not sign, and may not share their enthusiasm for their specialty. General education teachers, on the other hand, expected their principals to understand their work, and like any professionally trained adult, resented being told what to do. These teachers opposed mainstreaming because they had always been left out of planning and felt very distanced from placement decisions made at a higher level. In addition, of course, having deaf children in their classes was regarded as a burden that increased their workload, caused interruptions in the school day, and allowed another adult (the interpreter) into their classroom territory.

The current school principal, Mr. Johnson, had no special knowledge of deaf education. He was a more teacher-friendly manager, however, and made certain that the receiving teachers wanted deaf children in their classes. He also provided Mrs. Rogers, the second-grade mainstreaming teacher, a covert but not insignificant "bonus." Because Mrs. Rogers had five hard of hearing and deaf children in her classroom for half of each school day, she had a much smaller class of hearing second graders in the mornings. Most of the teachers understood why Mrs. Rogers had only twenty-three children in her second-grade class rather than the thirty to thirty-five that was the norm.

Finally, several teachers told me that mainstreaming was "so good for the normal children." This is a not an original point of view. Just after PL 94-142 was implemented, Brill (1978) noted the same theme in discussions of integrated classes. At Aspen School this belief was alive and well, and Mrs. Rogers reported that some parents of hearing children annually requested that their children be assigned to the mainstreaming classrooms because, in Mrs. Rogers' words, "they want their children to have that experience, of being with the handicapped and working with them in a normal classroom."

Each member of the general school staff had a comment, anecdote, or opinion about mainstreaming and about having deaf students in their school. Not surprisingly, virtually all of them named the sign language interpreters as the most visible feature of mainstreaming. In addition, many explained mainstreaming using easily recognized ideals like "providing equal educational opportunities for all." More than once the law was interpreted for me, and I learned what was "legally required" in a mainstream program for deaf children (e.g., music classes for deaf children) and what was "against the law" (e.g., permitting a deaf child to go to the restroom without an interpreter). Most of these informal conversations ended with the familiar claim that mainstreaming offered a beneficial experience to hearing children.

School staff who were more closely involved in mainstreaming (including the children's mainstreaming teachers, the instructional assistants, and specialist staff like the librarian and PE teacher) also repeatedly expressed two complex ideas. Their comments clearly and poignantly demonstrate the ways Aspen School attempted to achieve the mainstreaming ideals promoted by federal legislation (e.g., PL 94-142) and simultaneously created practice-related dilemmas. The first theme centered on "equality." The second was the troublesome notion of the "least restrictive environment."

IS IT EQUAL?

Teachers and support staff at Aspen School firmly believed that the school should strive to be equal (as opposed to differentially better or worse) for all the children, although it was not always clear what "equal" would look like in practice. The most common view at Aspen School was that the best way to promote equal education was to acknowledge the deaf children's civil rights: They had a right to be in a school with hearing children and to be placed in activities with them. Yet all of the teachers involved with the deaf children struggled with this rather abstract notion. Many of the staff characterized mainstreaming as a practice that has to do with civil rights or with providing an equal education. Others were careful to emphasize the difference between providing an education and providing the opportunity for an education, a distinction that turned out to be critical to district administrators.

Accordingly, in subtle ways the staff as a whole tended to regard the deaf children as students whose most pressing special educational characteristic was their right to be at Aspen School and not at a segregated school or an institution. In fact, this was virtually the only way the general education staff could grasp the idea of mainstreaming since none of them had any knowledge of the depth of deaf children's need for a fine-tuned education. Upholding the ideal of equal education defined the deaf children as practically normal (and completely normal when the interpreter was there) students who had a right to be among the hearing students and in general education classes. More or less unintentionally, this shifted the focus away from the educational implications of being deaf. This, of course, was very distressing to the teachers of the deaf, who juggled their ideals about equal access to education with their experience in and their beliefs about teaching deaf children. Ms. Roberts and Ms. Adams, who knew very well how far their deaf students lagged in basic skills, felt that mainstreaming compromised the children's already shaky status as learners at the school.

Although virtually all of the staff mentioned equality, the concept is an elusive one, and teachers tended to provide similar examples as concrete evidence of equality. For most of the general education teachers at Aspen School, equal educational opportunity was exemplified by deaf and hearing children playing together at recess. Most of the teachers genuinely believed that the deaf and hearing children played together at recess, although in reality, the children most often played in segregated groups (deaf/hearing, girls/boys, noisy/quiet, and so on). Further, Mrs. Rogers supported her belief that the hearing children did not consider the deaf children different from themselves with her observation that they were not unkind toward the deaf children. In this case, her observations were accurate. Even though intentional unkindness was not noticed in the mainstreaming classroom, it is nevertheless a challenge to see how these sentimental observations could constitute genuine evidence of the success of mainstreaming.

Mrs. Rogers had a personal policy about the deaf children, which she reported as "I don't pamper them, but I don't want them to be ignored." This reflected her ambivalence about exactly how to offer all her students equal educational opportunity. Noting the not uncommon dilemma of teaching a group of thirty children but needing (and wanting) to evaluate and guide each child's development, she remarked that she ultimately resolved this quandary by considering all of her students, deaf and hearing, as individuals. She recognized that all of her students had their own "personalities," sets of traits that naturally influenced the ways they engaged with school. Mrs. Rogers' kindness in the classroom and her virtually perfect distribution of turns during lessons (she was careful not to leave students out when they bid for turns and made a special effort to call on the deaf students) suggest her genuine respect for children and for the variety of skills and abilities they present. Reflecting on the pleasure she took in teaching, she commented, "Children are children. They are all special."

Her respect for the specialness of all children and her accompanying belief in the role of their personalities in determining their school behavior could take her only so far toward dealing with the deaf students, however. They exhibited traits that made them unlike the other children. They did not make eye contact with her, for instance, but watched the interpreter, a situation that she told me she could never get used to. The deaf children were distributed around the room, seated at tables with hearing students, and often had brief signed conversations when they should have been paying attention to her lessons. Tom, especially, had a hard time sitting still and was easily distracted. She tended to interpret the deaf children's behavior according to her model of "children as children." Like the other mainstreaming teachers, she knew very little about deaf children, and her model of the child took hearing children, her only real frame of reference, as the norm.

As she tried to explain the deaf children to me, she repeatedly placed them in the frames that made sense for hearing children. For instance, all children display varying desires to communicate with others: "[S]ome are more outgoing than others." She named one of the hearing children, who was very quiet and tended to keep to himself, and contrasted him with Robbie, who was frequently chided for trying to sign with the other deaf boys across the room during her lessons. She hypothesized that Robbie would probably be a very talkative boy "if he could talk." Continuing, she described Tom, a fidgety child, as an "enigma." She accounted for his apparent problems engaging with instruction in the mainstreaming classroom by wondering if he slept enough and if he ate properly. Children who act like Tom, she confided, often consume too much refined sugar. In the same vein, she recalled a difficult deaf student from the previous year, stating that even if this child were hearing, he would be "hyper." However, a great deal of the deaf children's lack of engagement was due to the organization of discourse in the classroom (discussed later), the pacing of the lesson, and the use of audiovisual equipment that left the room quite dark and required the children to look rapidly between a screen, the interpreter, and their work sheets.

Mrs. Rogers was an affectionate, efficient, and very trustworthy teacher. The description of her point of view is not intended as a criticism. In fact, her interpretations of the deaf children are partially correct: Tom often stayed up late and refused to eat many wholesome foods, and Robbie routinely took advantage of opportunities to communicate with others. Her outlook serves solely to point out the extent to which the ideal of equality in itself is insufficient to prepare teachers to take into account the seriousness of deaf children's need for comprehensible communication, that is, for specialized teaching that is difficult to enact in a regular classroom.

At Aspen School, placements were arranged to ensure that deaf children were sometimes in rooms with hearing children, and most teachers, and certainly the district administration and the school principal, felt that this constituted mainstreaming. Yet the lack of knowledge about deaf children and their learning needs created a situation where general education teachers were unable to get to know their deaf students and failed to help them learn.

Ms. Roberts and Ms. Adams were not pleased with the practical problems and confusions engendered by their colleagues' approach to including deaf children in their classes. They believed that general education staff did not take seriously enough the everyday problems of communication and engagement the deaf children encountered in the mainstream. From their points of view, elementary-age deaf children needed special support acquiring basic skills. Just as the general education staff felt that their obligation was to allow deaf children into their classes, the teachers of the deaf felt that their obligation was to provide the special, fine-tuned support their students needed in order to get a good start on their school careers.

Accordingly, they did not agree that equality of educational opportunity was the deaf children's dominant need. Neither of them spoke of equality, although they acknowledged this as the ultimate goal for deaf adults and the Deaf community. Rather, the two teachers of the deaf took as their starting place the importance of devising innovative practices for helping deaf children learn, an objective that mainstreaming often interfered with. Ms. Adams felt that the Aspen School mainstreaming program placed too much importance on trying to "normalize the deaf kids," that is, to consider them approximations of hearing children without addressing their special needs. Ms. Roberts took issue with the school policy that all deaf children should be mainstreamed unless they absolutely could not be, again pointing out what she felt was the general misunderstanding of deaf children's learning needs.

Mainstreaming placed burdens on general education teachers and created logistical problems for the teachers of the deaf as well. Highly orchestrated, fluid schedules are required for individual children in a public school mainstreaming program. As head teacher, Ms. Roberts negotiated schedules—a very time-consuming task—with the general education mainstreaming teachers. During a typical week, the deaf children had to be in up to nine different school settings with different adults (not including their bus drivers and unscheduled visits to the school health aid).

Ms. Roberts and Ms. Adams also had to reabsorb into the self-contained class the deaf children who could no longer be mainstreamed, those who exhibited perceived behavior problems. Regular teachers sometimes had legitimate reasons for requesting removal of a deaf student. Often, however, deaf students were removed for acting like deaf children: turning around in their chairs to converse with other deaf children or looking at the interpreter rather than the teacher and thus appearing to be inattentive. In addition, several of the mainstreaming teachers refused to administer even routine classroom discipline when a deaf child pushed another child, chewed gum, or refused to participate in classroom cleanup. Mrs. Rogers did not hesitate to discipline the deaf children, but other mainstreaming teachers sent misbehaving deaf children back to the self-contained classroom with a note describing their infraction. Ms. Roberts or Ms. Adams was expected to resolve the problem. Ironically, deaf children who persisted in acting very unlike hearing children (i.e., who acted like deaf signing children) were often removed from contact with hearing children altogether. Although, as in many mainstreaming situations, there was great faith in the power of hearing children to provide normal models for socializing the deaf children, the power of normal models apparently had limits. No one at Aspen School could socialize the deaf children so they would comport themselves like hearing children.

IS IT ACCESSIBLE EDUCATION?

The second element of equal education access is education. Although the deaf children's placements in mainstreaming settings provided the physical arrangement, the participants, and the discourse patterns of a school, in many ways these elements were of minimal educational benefit. The Aspen School community's pride in and enjoyment of their interpreters reflected their belief that providing interpreters was all that was necessary to open educational opportunities for young deaf children. Indeed, interpreters were actually the only adjustment made in the mainstreaming classrooms, although of course they were regarded as integral players in the mainstreaming program.

However, as Ms. Roberts, Ms. Adams, and Mrs. Hart well knew, simply providing an interpreter, even a very skilled native signer, was not sufficient to create equitable educational circumstances for deaf children. The teachers all felt strongly that the "hearing format" (Ms. Roberts's term for the traditional classroom discourse practices of the Aspen School teachers) added to the burden the deaf children shouldered when they tried to learn and participate in mainstreaming classrooms. They knew, for example, that deaf children cannot watch an interpreter and simultaneously read a text, do a math problem, correct a spelling word, or draw a picture. In-service training and much individual advising was offered to mainstreaming teachers. However, Aspen School was organized for hearing children on the whole, not for deaf children. The classroom interpreters sometimes had to ask teachers to speak more slowly, to allow only one speaker at a time, and to avoid speaking when their backs were to the class. These are difficult adjustments to maintain, although Mrs. Rogers always complied when Mrs. Hart reminded her. More seriously, even when asked to do so by the teachers of the deaf, the mainstreaming teachers made little or no effort to reorganize their presentation of materials in the mainstreaming settings. The "chalk-and-talk" discourse pattern, where the teacher speaks while writing examples on the board or pointing to texts, was the most common instruction method.

Mrs. Hart's perspective on this problem was particularly poignant since she had grown up as a struggling hard of hearing student, was ethnically deaf, and was the interpreter (hence, always present) in the mainstreaming second-grade classroom. She believed that mainstreaming teachers routinely used the interpreter to "remove themselves from the situation." Teachers avoided engaging with deaf children in several ways. First, they could simply ignore them, fail to respond to their bids for turns, and never offer them a chance to participate. It would be naive to say that this never occurs in integrated settings. Second, they could overtly or covertly relinquish their authority as a teacher, direct the interpreter to attend to or help the deaf child, and never interact with the child. Although this too is far removed from the goals of integration, it certainly happens. Mrs. Hart noted that she and the other interpreters were often regarded as inanimate classroom tools, like "pieces of chalk." She was very willing to occupy the interpreter niche in the elementary classrooms, a role that is very different from interpreting for deaf adults in noneducational settings. However, she felt that the teachers must also occupy their proper niche, that of general education teacher with deaf children in the room. Their obligations consisted of properly using the interpreter, interacting with and teaching the deaf students, and recognizing that the interpreters are people.

Mrs. Hart was directly confronted many times with the contrast between the general Aspen School pride at providing interpreters and individual teachers' lack of faith in both the abilities of deaf children and the capacity of signing genuinely to convey meaning. She recalled one teacher who expressed her doubts that deaf children could really learn anything through signing. This teacher abdicated her own responsibility for evaluating a particular deaf child's learning by ignoring the child's work and instead asking Mrs. Hart for her assessment of the child. Had she actually learned anything that year in the mainstreaming class?

Since Mrs. Hart had raised deaf children of her own and had dealt with schools and teachers for many years as a mother of both a residential school student and a mainstreaming program student, her personal goals for mainstreaming were especially touching. When discussing mainstreaming, she never mentioned equality as a motivator, although she held fierce opinions about civil rights and self-determination for Deaf people. Instead, she summed up interpreting in educational settings:

> "I have to go by my opinion, my philosophy, my personality, and what I hope to God was given to my children when they were mainstreamed . . . [a]nd if somebody doesn't educate them, if somebody doesn't give them all the advantages and help and everything . . . well, who will?"

In addition to difficulties that arose from the chalk-and-talk format of the class, in the mainstreaming class the deaf children had severely reduced opportunities to communicate. They had three academic subjects in the mainstreaming class—math, social studies, and science; of these three, social studies and math were often previewed and/or reviewed in the self-contained class. The children had a second-grade science book, but the frequently hands-on lessons focused on plants, animals, and weather. By coincidence, these topics were sometimes discussed in the self-contained classroom, but there was no intentional preteaching. The other mainstreaming activities—recess, lunch, PE, music, art, and visits to the library—were certainly subjects in which the deaf children should have had genuine opportunities to participate. Interpreters were again present but unable to manage the task of re-creating contexts for hearing children so that deaf children could participate.

TOO MUCH EQUALITY

The adults at Aspen School apparently—although not surprisingly—had a hard time reconciling their ideals with everyday life teaching deaf children in mainstreaming settings. However, the atmosphere in the school reflected more than confusion. At Aspen School, the goal of creating a situation where all the children were equal created an ideological trap into which some of the hearing staff, including some mainstreaming teachers, fell. The pressure to overlook the genuine differences between deaf and hearing children, especially the deaf children's distinctive way of communicating, created the illusion that all the children in the school had been rendered equal. Accordingly, the fact that the deaf children received any special or separate treatment at all (beyond the one acceptable adjustment—the interpreter) was evidence, from some teachers' point of view, that they had unfairly managed to obtain more equality, or a higher quality education, than the hearing students. During the school year, the sentiment among general education staff grew to such a degree that some made the exaggerated claim that the deaf children discriminated against the hearing children because they enjoyed extra privileges.

Yet the time they spent in the self-contained classroom, where their basic literacy lessons were conducted, was by its nature separate, and the deaf children participated in separate and different activities with their deaf classmates and staff of the hearing impaired program. Although one might expect that a teacher with thirty hearing children and no instructional assistants would resent the more favorable teacher-student ratio in the self-contained classroom, other manifestations of the belief that deaf children enjoyed "extra equality" were more problematic.

For example, Ms. Adams reported that some of the staff believed that the deaf children had more rights, tipping the scale of equality in their favor. It was especially resented that they went on extra "field trips," which in reality were visits to an audiology clinic for hearing tests. The most hotly contested extra "privilege" during the school day, however, was seating in the lunchroom. That this seemingly trivial matter had been a problem at the school for at least two years illustrated the genuine distance between the deaf and hard of hearing program and the rest of Aspen School.

Children at Aspen School had a brief lunch period (between fifteen and twenty minutes). Filing into the cafeteria by class and according to a staggered schedule, they were assigned to a table. The school principal believed that this lunch schedule and seating arrangement ensured a smooth running lunch period that was adequate for the children to eat but not long enough for them to get into trouble. This schedule also made for smaller groups of students in the cafeteria at a time, promoting groups that were easier to monitor and therefore safer for all the children. Because children who had friends or siblings in other classes could not eat lunch with them under this plan, complaints about this system were routine. The deaf children went to lunch with their mainstreaming classes and sat with them at their assigned table.

Purportedly to forestall kicking, all children were seated on only one side of the table. The rule was that a student had to take the first seat that was available when he or she arrived at the table. As a result, none of the children faced anyone as they sat at the long lunchroom tables. They did not necessarily get to sit next to or even near their closest friends, especially if one friend had "cold lunch" (and sat down immediately) and the other bought "hot lunch" (and sat down after waiting in line). Children who did not quickly strategize and organize themselves as they lined up to enter the cafeteria did not get to choose their lunch partners. This arrangement was quite unpopular with the children, who liked to sit with friends during lunch. The principal's reasoning in response to complaints was that lunchtime was for eating, not for socializing, which the children should save for recess or for after school.

Mrs. Hart, Ms. Roberts, and Ms. Adams had observed how easily the deaf children became marooned during lunch, with no one to converse with and no one to be with "kid style" (the term Mrs. Hart used for peer interaction). Further, they noted that it was harder for deaf children to communicate with their tablemates than it was for hearing children since the deaf children had to be able to see their interlocutors. They asked if students could be seated on both sides of the table and were turned down. They did finally arrange permission for the deaf children to sit next to each other if they wished at their mainstream class's table.

Robbie, Tom, and Paul sat at the table assigned to Mrs. Rogers' second-grade class, but they were allowed to sit with each other rather than taking the next available seat. This seemingly sensible solution to the problem of providing a minimal opportunity to communicate with other children during lunchtime caused many hard feelings among the other teachers. This was evidence, they felt, of the worst possible outcome of special education for deaf children: The youngsters were intentionally isolating themselves from the others, becoming "ghettoized," the exact opposite of the intentions of the law and a denigration of the ideals of integration and equality. But the fact that the deaf children could sit with their friends produced the most displeasure and was used to bolster the argument that the deaf children were discriminating against the hearing children by enjoying extra privileges.

The unveiled resentment of the deaf children's lunchroom and field trip arrangements disturbed Ms. Roberts and Ms. Adams, who generously interpreted the schoolwide attitude as evidence that "hearing people just don't understand." They also believed that there was a great deal about deafness, deaf children, and the culture of Deaf people that hearing people could not possibly have had an opportunity to learn. However, both teachers as well as Mrs. Hart expressed concern that the deaf children were being punished for being deaf in the mainstreaming settings.

In the lunchroom, even when seated next to another signing child, the deaf children were still in an inconvenient and uncomfortable arrangement for signing. They sometimes squirmed on the bench or stood up in order to see their interlocutors. These physical actions were interpreted by the lunchroom monitors as violations of a lunchroom rule— the requirement to sit still. The deaf students were then disciplined for taking action to meet their needs as people who communicated by signing.

Similar problems arose in the mainstreaming classrooms when teachers instructed classes to look at their books while the teachers continued lecturing. The deaf students either looked down a few moments later (after they had received the interpreted instruction) or refrained from looking down at all in order to continue watching the interpreter. Several such instances occurred where teachers interpreted the deaf children's actions as disrespectful rather than as sensible solutions to the problem of using interpreters in situations designed for people with intact hearing.

The ideal of equality is not sufficient in itself to help teachers differentiate between the crucial differences that deaf children present in the classroom from the many ways that they appear to be like other children. The tension between the ideal and the reality of life in a school with such different kinds of children, deaf and hearing, integrated with each other was genuine and difficult to surmount.

These observations do not fault any individual or school. Rather, they illustrate the ways that mainstreaming can play out in daily life when the situation is incompletely defined and the needs of students poorly understood. Although the Aspen School program clearly reflected the idealized goals of legislation promoting education for all children with disabilities, defining deaf children as children whose most pressing needs were protection of their rights and inclusion with "normal" children overlooked the educational implications of their deafness. The illusion that the deaf children were only marginally different from other children at the school created conflicts and bad feelings among the staff. In addition, it also did nothing actually to help the children learn the basic skills and school subjects the school was obligated to teach them in the mainstreaming settings.

REALITY

Least Restrictive Environment

The Aspen School community responded to the mainstreaming program in their midst by turning to the idealized goal of equality. In practice, however, this goal was difficult to achieve. The efforts of teachers to locate and implement LREs for the deaf children did not necessarily ensure the children's complete access to school.

One seemingly practical guideline for constructing equal educational opportunity is provided in the implementation guidelines for PL 94-142, which state that "to the maximum extent appropriate" children with handicaps should be educated with able-bodied children with normal hearing. Although this appears to favor mainstreaming classrooms such as Mrs. Rogers's room at Aspen School, such a placement is *not* required by the law. However, the notion of LRE is sufficiently confusing that in practice it is generally interpreted as requiring schooling in integrated settings to the greatest extent possible (Commission 1988). Although the guidelines also require specially designed instruction to meet each child's needs and related services that may be necessary to achieve educational goals, implementation of these was not as troublesome as the LRE at Aspen School. Instruction in the self-contained classes responded to the first goal, and interpreters, communication disorders specialists, and the itinerant school counselor constituted the second.

Communications between district offices and the Aspen School teachers of the deaf suggested that at the district level, special education staff regarded placement in the LRE, translated as "integrated settings," as more important than communication and educational goals for the deaf children. As a result, general education teachers also held strong opinions about the best placements for deaf children and expressed them freely. Between teachers of the deaf and mainstreaming teachers the placement issue was often framed in terms of territoriality, especially the legitimate "ownership" of the deaf children. In addition, there were tensions over the logistics of creating and maintaining LREs in schools: the physical, spatial, and temporal details of life based on the desire to integrate deaf and hearing children in the same classroom and the same school.

Where Do the Deaf Children Belong?

Ms. Roberts and Ms. Adams shared Mrs. Hart's sentiments about educating deaf children. In essence all three women felt that they must see to the details of their students' early school years, especially their ability to communicate with others. They were the best trained to do this, and their experience working in a public school led them to believe that no one else would or could do it. Although they accepted the idea that mainstreaming was an integral part of the hearing impaired program offered by their district, most often they discussed their work as helping deaf children to develop and to learn by trying to devise ways to teach them to read, write, and spell English, by providing an intelligible setting for interaction so that the children could gain competence in ASL, and by helping them learn about the world, including the lives of Deaf people. Hence, concerns about equality were not foremost in their minds and not an immediate elementary school goal. All three of them, however, felt that a solid foundation based upon signing ASL, English print literacy, and knowledge of the subject areas of the early school years would promote both educational and vocational equality over the course of their students' lives.

For example, Ms. Roberts, Ms. Adams, and Mrs. Hart all mentioned how important it was for the deaf children to realize that they were as good as hearing children, that hearing children did not have any secrets that the deaf children could not discover, and that they could compete with them and be in the same world with them. They hoped that the deaf students would grow into people who could function in many settings and make sense of hearing people and the expectations of the hearing world. At the same time, they recognized a crucial but surprisingly elusive fact about deaf children. Ms. Roberts stated that for the deaf students "there's still certainly the sense of not being the same as hearing kids." That is, Ms. Roberts knew that they were not, and never would be, hearing children.

This fact was apparent to the deaf children as well. Although the second graders had a broader definition of *deaf* than most hearing adults do, they clearly understood that they were deaf and that they would be deaf when they got older. Their current hypotheses about who was deaf also included hearing adults whom they knew and liked and who signed, and excluded their peers in the self-contained classroom who used hearing aids but did not sign. (Tom's, Robbie's, and Paul's notions about who was deaf and who was hearing factored into their understanding of literacy and are discussed in more detail in Ramsey, in press).

Because of their training and experience, the teachers in the self-contained classroom understood that deaf children needed a specially designed education in elementary school. At the very least, they believed that special attention must be devoted to communication and to language learning. They all felt that their primary responsibility was to provide this specially designed education in their classroom for the deaf children. Although in reality their attention was diverted by many duties beyond teaching, they tried to devote their professional attention to this part of their program. Both Ms. Roberts and Ms. Adams reported that they spent a great deal of energy doing "public relations" on behalf of the deaf students and making concessions to the mainstreaming teachers in order to make things (i.e., inclusion of the deaf children) easier for them. Both lamented that—since they had so many other duties—they did not have enough genuine teaching time with the deaf students.

In contrast, the regular staff at Aspen School lacked training and experience in both education of deaf children and in the management of mainstreaming. There was virtually no preparation provided by the school for the mainstreaming teachers. Teachers could, on their own time and at their own expense, take a weekend workshop on children with disabilities; annually, the teachers of the deaf provided a ten-lesson sign language workshop after school for students and for teachers. Beyond this, mainstreaming teachers had little understanding of the ways the deaf and hard of hearing program provided specially designed education for deaf children. Since this fact was not foremost in their minds, they did not comprehend many of the ways that the self-contained classroom might constitute the central context for the deaf children's learning. Their only recourse was to focus their attention on equality and the practical construction of equality via the notion of the LRE.

Mrs. Rogers, for example, had no special preparation for being the mainstreaming teacher of deaf children. Although she planned to take a weekend workshop on integrating children with disabilities and although she had read a book on generic standards, she recognized that her knowledge was very general. In fact, one of her greatest fears was that mainstreaming would eventually lead to the end of special education and the resulting placement of all children with disabilities into regular classrooms. She was especially concerned that she might become responsible for medically frail children and worried that she would have to handle medical equipment like catheters. "I'm not a nurse. If something went wrong, would I be responsible?" she asked with concern.

In practical terms, Mrs. Rogers understood that the LRE was a legal guideline for providing deaf children access to educational settings. Despite her respect for the law, she recognized the practical factors that intervened. She knew very well that at Aspen School, not all teachers graciously welcomed deaf children and an interpreter in their classrooms. The barest structure of an LRE depended to a great degree on the receiving teacher's inclination to accept this responsibility.

Mrs. Rogers herself had struggled to learn to work with Mrs. Hart and felt that adding five deaf and hard of hearing children to her classroom every day was possible but just barely so. She knew that other teachers were not willing to make the same adjustments. Although she believed that regular classrooms with hearing children genuinely provided an LRE, she could easily imagine that many regular teachers might be unable or unwilling to handle mainstreaming.

Like Mrs. Rogers, Ms. Roberts's comments on achieving equal educational opportunity for deaf students through the LRE reflected the tension between guarding the civil rights of deaf children and providing them with an education. She echoed the Aspen School community's received legalistic sentiments when she stated that "time in mainstreaming settings is not something that deaf kids have to earn." In other words, the school had an obligation to provide integration with hearing children to the extent it was possible and appropriate.

In practice, however, Ms. Roberts had to devote energy to "selling" the deaf children to the hearing teachers. More seriously, she had to live with her own conviction that provision of education in the least restrictive environment did not constitute the optimal arrangement for fostering deaf children's learning in the early years of school. One day after a conversation with a representative of the district office, she lamented: "We're not required to provide the ultimate program, but an *adequate* program. Not the best."

During an interview, Ms. Roberts reported her attempts to explain to administrators and other teachers that deaf children needed intensive and early attention to language development and communication so that they could have access to the tools necessary to develop basic skills. She stated that it was not likely that such attention could be provided if young deaf children were placed for hours at a time in mainstreaming settings. (Not only was she critical of mainstreaming, but she also held strong and at the time unconventional views on deaf education pedagogy since she believed that deaf children's early education was best accomplished through ASL.) She had been told by her superiors that deaf children only had to "make it" in mainstreaming classrooms, and if they could make it (i.e., not fail every evaluation), then the practice was worth the children's time.

Ms. Adams's comments reflected similar sentiments. She understood that the teachers at Aspen School generally believed that mainstreaming was the best setting for "normalizing" deaf children. From workshops, newsletters, teacher meetings, and the popular press, the teachers had all learned that regular classrooms were, by definition, less restrictive and that such classes were beneficial for children with disabilities. (There was also a widespread belief that mainstreaming was beneficial for hearing students.) Ms. Adams conceded that mainstreaming might have merit, but given the way it was organized at Aspen School, she asked, "What's the point of mainstreaming? Wouldn't it be nice if we could structure it differently?" She believed, for example, that the whole program could be enhanced if they could work more closely and plan in more detail with the mainstreaming teachers. Under the current organization, there was simply no time for such close collaboration. In addition, mainstreaming teachers were sometimes unwilling or unable to engage in detailed planning with the teachers of the deaf.

Differing notions of mainstreaming and education of deaf children spawned heated discussions over where the deaf children belonged within the school building. Both sets of teachers regarded the deaf children almost as possessions. "Ownership" was regularly broached in the hallway and in teachers' room conversations as well as during brief planning meetings in comments like "she's my student" or "they're enrolled in my class." Ms. Roberts and Ms. Adams regarded their self-contained classroom as the core of the deaf children's school experience. During mainstreaming hours the deaf children were outside of their genuine setting, at best actually learning math or other subjects and at worst, marooned in an unstimulating environment with limited avenues for participating in class and few people they could communicate with.

After two years of working as the second-grade mainstreaming teacher, Mrs. Rogers had formulated a similar view of the deaf children, at least of Robbie, Paul, and Tom. They were regular visitors to whom she had a responsibility, whom she did not fully understand, and for whom she tried to remember to make special adjustments. Despite their physical integration with the hearing second graders, Mrs. Rogers realized that the deaf boys were each other's "true friends" and noted that signing together was "part of their world where they are real comfortable."

In contrast, other school staff, including some of the mainstreaming teachers, expressed an opposing view. In line with their claim that the whole school was accessible, they held that the mainstreaming classrooms constituted the core of the deaf children's school experience. For instance, the third- and fourth-grade mainstreaming teachers believed that the deaf children's names should appear on the rosters of the regular classes and that they should report to these classes first thing in the morning. In their view, the deaf students should be pulled out of the mainstream for special attention in the self-contained classroom rather than the opposite scenario. Several general education teachers went so far as to state that the teachers of the deaf were merely special education teachers whose expertise extended only to hearing aid technology and the discipline and behavior management of deaf children. Only regular teachers, they claimed, were real teachers who knew how to teach children.

These ownership issues contributed to the schoolwide ambivalence about the mainstreaming program and its purpose. For example, the deaf children had calendar time each morning with their teachers and classmates in the self-contained classroom. Like many teachers, Ms. Roberts, Ms. Adams, and Mrs. Hart believed that a sense of community was important for the children in their classroom, and they used the early mornings for fostering such a feeling. Through their morning rituals, they had built a shared history that endured over several school years for some of their students, as well as a strong sense of friendship among the deaf children.

Because the general education teachers also used morning rituals and special events for similar purposes, there were disagreements about where the deaf children should go first thing in the morning. Unfortunately, these discordant points of view dissolved into trivializing arguments about where the children should hang their coats and store their lunch bags. Although these disagreements were eventually resolved (most of the deaf children went to the self-contained classroom first thing in the morning), the fact that they arose in the first place reflected again the difficult and inevitable details of managing a mainstreaming program for deaf children in a public school.

Interestingly, the deaf children claimed both classrooms. They reported that the self-contained classroom and the mainstreaming classrooms were both their class, and they named all of the adults—Ms. Adams, Ms. Roberts, Mrs. Rogers, and sometimes Mrs. Hart—when asked who their teacher was. However, all three of the boys, and all but one of the other deaf second- and third-graders reported that they preferred the self-contained classroom. Since the self-contained and mainstreaming classrooms were organized quite differently, there were many reasons for this preference. However, when asked to elaborate about the mainstreaming classroom and the hearing children, Robbie stated patiently, "I am deaf," and explained the obvious fact that people in the self-contained classroom could sign and people in the mainstreaming class could not.

Logistics of Communication

Given the physical, spatial, and temporal reality of school life, logistical problems constituted a second outgrowth of attempts to create a least restrictive environment for the deaf children. As used here, logistics is a broad category that includes some of the everyday practices, problems, and adjustments that mainstreaming teachers, teachers of the deaf, and interpreters needed to recognize and to tackle. The focus of these adjustments was the attention that must be paid to communication between deaf and hearing people.

The adjustments to classroom life brought about by integration of deaf children with hearing children were most burdensome on the mainstreaming teachers. Not surprisingly, after the ideal of equality, the second recurring topic in discussions with Mrs. Rogers was the basic set of dilemmas inherent in accepting into her classroom children who could not hear. In part because of her great respect for the hard won civil rights of students with disabilities, Mrs. Rogers was very willing to accept the deaf children into her classroom. However, her sense of civic responsibility did not blind her to the practical problems that mainstreaming introduced into her life as a teacher.

In addition to the disruption caused when the deaf children and Mrs. Hart moved in and out of the classroom, Mrs. Rogers lost some flexibility and spontaneity in her daily planning. The deaf children were scheduled to arrive at specific times each day, which corresponded to specific subjects. Responsible for teaching several important subjects to the deaf children—math, social studies and science—Mrs. Rogers took her obligation seriously.

However, the contents of a school day sometimes overflow the vessel of the schedule. Occasionally a particularly timely or interesting *Weekly Reader* would arrive or a long-awaited film would finally appear. At other times she and the children would become involved in an especially productive discussion or an enjoyable reading or art project. At these moments Mrs. Rogers could not simply adjust the schedule to take advantage of the children's pleasure or her own feeling of success. When the deaf children arrived, her obligation was to teach math.

Ms. Roberts and Ms. Adams felt the scheduling burdens also, although in a different way. By tradition, they were the ones who had to plan their days and weeks around the mainstreaming teachers' plans, which were regarded as primary and too difficult to adjust later. As a result, their days—and hence the deaf students' days—tended to be fragmented. Not all mainstreaming teachers were as conscientious as Mrs. Rogers was about adhering to the schedule. For all the teachers, however, the most serious adjustments involved attempts to reorganize communication in the classroom. These included first providing and using interpreters and, second, attending to virtually unconscious features of classroom discourse: the structure, organization, and management of "teacher talk" (Heath 1978). As interpreters know, it is very difficult to focus on the latter during ongoing discourse. An interpreter can ask speakers to slow down, and they often do so when reminded. However, few speakers can sustain careful and reflective attention to the pace of speech and also continue rapidly participating in discourse in real time.

Both Mrs. Rogers and Mrs. Hart recalled their first year of working together as mainstreaming teacher and interpreter, respectively. Mrs. Hart reported that it took a year for her to get accustomed to working with a mainstreaming teacher. If she had the opportunity to work with one teacher for two years in a row, the patterns of the teacher and classroom became habitual, and the classes proceeded, in Mrs. Hart's terms, "like clockwork." One feature of the awkward first year was that Mrs. Rogers, a hearing woman who did not sign, had to make a leap of faith. She had to trust that signing could actually work to accomplish communication and that interpreting in both directions between spoken English and signing was possible. According to Mrs. Hart, not all teachers successfully negotiated the leap. In her experience, many nonsigning teachers simply did not trust sign language interpreters. She stated, "I really believe that hearing people think that when we sign we are just doing absolutely zilch, that we don't know what we are doing. . . . I'm in their domain, and there's someone there doing something they can't understand." Mrs. Rogers reflected a similar sentiment, recalling the beginning of her first year as a mainstreaming teacher, when she tried to teach her classes with interpreters "even though I didn't know what [the interpreters] were doing."

The organization of territory and space in Mrs. Rogers' class constituted another prominent feature of interpreting. Mrs. Hart was well aware that the mainstreaming teachers found it awkward that she stood or sat near them in their accustomed space in front of the class. Mrs. Rogers spoke of the adjustment she had to make when Mrs. Hart first joined her. Having devoted some thought to seating arrangements so that the deaf children had a clear line of vision to Mrs. Hart, Mrs. Rogers nevertheless felt that she no longer knew where to stand in her own classroom. She often found herself "between the deaf child and the interpreter," an apt description of mainstreaming teachers' distance from the deaf children.

By far the most serious difficulty with using an interpreter in the second-grade classroom was organization of talk itself. Mrs. Rogers reported feeling vaguely uncomfortable and often dissatisfied with her teaching of the mixed group. Mrs. Rogers knew how to use a sign language interpreter, she knew the deaf children could not hear her speech, and she knew that they were as much her students as the hearing children. These were the facts of life in her classroom, and she recognized their immutability. Nonetheless, she reported that she had to "make a concentrated effort" to call on the deaf children. During lessons, their behavior, eye gaze, and often body shifts signaled that they were engaged with the interpreter. Rightly or wrongly, Mrs. Rogers interpreted these signals as lack of engagement with her, an interpretation of discourse that makes perfect sense. This distorted her patterns of interaction, especially with regard to distributing turns. Accordingly, despite her knowledge of their presence, the deaf students simply did not occupy the same status as the hearing students. Simply put, the hearing students were genuine participants and potential turn-takers in her class. The deaf students, because of the nature of interpreting and the very real facts of not hearing speech, were not.

In addition, Mrs. Rogers tried to remember to keep her face visible to the class at all times. Unaccustomed to this constraint, however, she often forgot and turned her back on the class as she continued speaking and writing on the chalk board. She also felt that alterations in the pacing of her speech and reorganization of topics, especially the introduction of new topics during lessons, were often necessary in order to reach all of her students. Although she sometimes felt her timing was off, she had not identified exactly why, only that it occurred when the deaf children were there. She suggested that her vague discomfort with pacing had to do with the school subjects she was presenting to the mixed class rather than with teaching via an interpreter to a class of children who presented unusually varied experience with print and very different kinds of knowledge about the world. Not surprisingly, given the minimal preparation and support she received as a mainstreaming teacher, Mrs. Rogers had no way to analyze her classroom situation and come to an understanding of her teaching predicament.

Although Mrs. Rogers perceived something amiss with her classroom timing, the fact that interpreting necessarily involved processing time (a lag of several seconds) between her utterances and Mrs. Hart's signing was not factored into her accounts of teaching deaf children. Rather, she mentioned that some subjects were not suitable for an integrated classroom, specifically language arts, parts of which had been experimentally included in mainstreaming the previous year. According to Mrs. Rogers, it was not possible to include deaf children in language arts periods, not because she did not have the necessary training to teach deaf children language but because the deaf students' "concept of language and using it" was so different from that of hearing students. In response to this, she proceeded much more slowly, and the alteration in pace distorted her teaching and slowed the pace for the whole class. As a result, language instruction was removed from the mainstreaming schedule. She conjectured that her oddly paced lessons with the current group of deaf children were a result of the features of science, social studies, and math that depended on language skill, certainly a true statement. However, the task of teaching through an interpreter also played a role, which Mrs. Rogers did not fully comprehend.

The general problems arising from communication between hearing teachers and deaf children through an interpreter weighed heavily on Mrs. Hart. According to her, despite the facts that she and Mrs. Rogers were accustomed to each other and the deaf and hearing children were used to being in the same room, there were still many times when communication "just broke down." She acknowledged several possible sources of the breakdown, beginning with a fact well known to interpreters in elementary schools. Like many young children, the deaf second-graders had variable attention spans and simply did not watch the interpreter at all times. Although the hearing children also had lapses of attention, those of the deaf children were more obvious, especially to Mrs. Hart, who scanned the room to look at their faces as she interpreted. Robbie, Paul, and especially Tom did not look at her, sometimes because they were confused or had lost their places on the page, sometimes because they simply tuned out, and sometimes because Mrs. Rogers moved around the room as she spoke, and the children decided to look at what she was doing rather than watch the interpreter. An interpreted education is very unlike interacting directly with a teacher, and the deaf children were naturally less engaged in the mainstreaming classroom than they were in the self-contained classroom.

In addition to such breakdowns initiated by the deaf boys, Mrs. Hart also reported that even well-meaning teachers persisted in reading to the children, lecturing, or conversing with them as they did their seatwork. That is, despite their in-service workshops and their experience with deaf children, mainstreaming teachers organized communication in the classroom as if all the students were hearing. They simply did not take into account on a conscious level that the deaf children could not hear speech. In fact, mainstreaming with an interpreter supported the illusion that the deaf children were not critically different after all and that having an interpreter rendered the deaf children virtually hearing. As a result, the deaf children could not have access to everything that the teachers said in the classroom.

Showing films in the classroom, another common elementary school activity, presented an interpreting challenge not only because they were fast paced. Films also presented interesting visual images—very attractive to all children. Furthermore, in a totally dark room the deaf children could not see Mrs. Hart well, even if they tried to. At other times, Mrs. Rogers darkened the room and stood in the back to speak as she used an overhead projector to project images onto a screen in front. The deaf children had to decide between watching Mrs. Rogers herself or looking at the screen. Mrs. Hart had to decide where to stand: in the conventional spot near the speaking, hearing person or near the spot where the children might look—the screen, for example. Most of the breakdowns, however, occurred because the spoken discourse and the bidding for and distribution of turns outpaced the interpreted version. Winston (1992) points out that features of communication and instruction in mainstreaming classrooms are often simply not "interpretable." Employing a sign language interpreter for elementary deaf students is far from the ideal solution to the challenges of teaching them. At Aspen School, not through ill will but through well-intentioned provision of support services, the mainstreaming placement was not intelligible to deaf children, despite the illusion of access.

Mrs. Hart considered Mrs. Rogers "a great teacher." However, she confided that there were "several teachers here that I'd just as soon forget that I'm supposed to go to." She characterized these teachers as "self-centered." They were not unwilling to accept the deaf children and the interpreter into their classrooms, but they simply did not take any further steps to include them. Furthermore, self-centered teachers were poor communicators who did not try to make the content of their messages clear and straightforward, who mumbled or did not face the class when they spoke, or who demanded that the deaf children look in two places at once. They made it much more difficult for Mrs. Hart to feel that she was doing a competent job. She felt that they did not trust what she was doing even though she repeatedly explained to them that "we [interpreters] are signing what you said."

The familiar tension between ideal and real runs through the problems with LREs and logistics at Aspen School. Just as respect for the ideal of equality does not translate into the achievement of equality, the efforts of teachers to locate and implement least restrictive placements for the deaf children did not necessarily result in unrestricted access to school.

The problems that accompanied mainstreaming at Aspen School suggest that organizing a school around legal guidelines designed to provide equal educational opportunity for deaf children is a task that presents many difficulties and few genuinely helpful solutions. At Aspen School there was a lack of preparation for mainstreaming, especially for teachers and hearing children. Because their needs were often misconstrued, there were minimal adjustments when the deaf children were included. The adjustments that were made were based more upon concerns about the deaf children's right to equal educational opportunity than to their need for special education based on unimpeded communication.

Most seriously, there was a widespread and unjustified belief that a kind of magic was created by the physical proximity of deaf and hearing children and the presence of an interpreter. Mrs. Hart believed that the hearing people at the school used the interpreters to avoid engaging with deaf children directly. Quite possibly the entire school (and perhaps many others facing the same situation) employs the presence of interpreters to evade the responsibility for devising education and integration of deaf and hearing children. (See Higgins 1990 and Banks 1994 for contrasting descriptions of mainstreaming programs and suggestions for solutions.)

Chapter 5

Peer Interaction and Communication

in the Least Restrictive Environment

The adults' ideals about mainstreaming and their dilemmas realizing them were always present at Aspen School although they were not always in the forefront. Everyone had a point of view, but teachers did not generally discuss mainstreaming. Not wishing to be more closely involved, most assumed that the deaf and hard of hearing program and the mainstreaming arrangements were taking care of themselves. Like Mrs. Rogers, many believed that the deaf and hearing children were friendly and kind to each other and played together at recess. Reality indicated otherwise, however, and suggested that features of communication between deaf and hearing peers in the mainstreaming classroom merited a closer look.

If the deaf and hearing children truly did play together and get along, how did they accomplish it, especially when the hearing children were not signers and the deaf students were not speakers of English? In addition, it is often claimed that deaf children benefit from the presence of normal models, who are especially helpful for increasing deaf children's communication abilities (especially their English competence) and strengthening their social skills (especially their potential assimilation with hearing people).

Mrs. Rogers organized instructional discourse in her classroom very traditionally. Although children sat in clusters of desks, instructional activities were not carried out in groups but by individual children who worked alone, in concert with Mrs. Rogers' spoken instruction. Other than Mrs. Rogers' lectures and exchanges with the children, very little talk occurred during math, science, and social studies instruction in her classroom. The students had one discourse obligation to fulfill: They were responders to teacher instructions, directives, and questions. Sometimes they responded by raising their hands and taking a turn. More often, they listened to a brief explanation and responded by doing a worksheet or a page of arithmetic problems. During seatwork, Mrs. Rogers circulated and presented questions, directives, and evaluations to individual students. As a class, then, second-graders in her room did not have abundant opportunities for using language face-to-face as part of their learning. In her very teacher-centered classroom, as Mrs. Rogers herself noted, any talk during instructional periods that was not directed by her was "underground" and against her rules. Accordingly, none of the students, hearing or deaf, were offered rich opportunities to engage in conversation with her. Despite Mrs. Rogers' best intention, conversations between her and individual deaf students using Mrs. Hart to interpret were rare.

Naturally, these strict classroom talking rules were frequently violated among peers, a fact that Mrs. Rogers recognized and selectively corrected. As a result, in the mainstreaming classroom, the richest source of spontaneous interaction for the deaf children was talk among peers. In addition to unofficial peer conversations, children were allowed to converse quietly with the others at their table during art—"rainy day (i.e., indoor) recess"—and during transitions between instructional activities, when routine teacher-directed classroom order was momentarily suspended.

Every afternoon Tom, Robbie, and Paul walked over to Mrs. Rogers' room and spent the rest of the school day with the hearing second-graders. This period usually included afternoon recess. The deaf boys filtered into the room, sometimes in a group and sometimes one by one, and went to their seats. Sometimes Mrs. Hart walked over with them; at other times, if she was interpreting somewhere else, she had to meet them there. If the math lesson had already begun, the boys had to get their bearings by looking around at their classmates, wait for Mrs. Rogers' help locating the correct page, or attend to Mrs. Hart as she interpreted for Mrs. Rogers and helped them catch up. Orienting themselves was not an easy task. For example, one day Robbie raised his hand and kept it up for over four minutes. When he was finally recognized, his question was "Where are we?" He had missed a large section of the worksheet they were going through because he had never figured out what Mrs. Rogers was talking about.

Very little interaction occurred in the second-grade classroom. When the deaf children were there, it was for instruction. Mrs. Rogers' pattern (one that seemed common in Aspen School and is conventional in American education in general) was to talk, call on children, write on the board or use other props (e.g., a large clock face), and refer often to the children's workbooks or worksheets. She also made use of films and objects the children could see or touch: maps, seeds, pinecones, mealworms, or shells. She was aware that this allowed little time or opportunity for official interaction among the children during math, science, and social studies. Her model of teaching did not include peer conversation, class discussions, or free time as helpful practices for young children. Rather, she felt an obligation to cover the second-grade material so that the children would be prepared for third grade.

During rainy day recess, quiet talk was allowed, although the children were supposed to stay in their seats. During art, the children could talk, and they also moved around the room getting supplies, consulting with other kids about their work, exhibiting their art, or storing their projects—setting clay figures on a shelf to dry, for example. During transitions, the children sometimes moved about the room, replacing materials, storing projects, or getting drinks of water.

Transitions were also times when an important event took place. Mrs. Rogers looked for a "quiet row" or "quiet table" and awarded "positive action" points or other privileges to the best behaved students. During this event the children in each group tried to urge the others to hurry, sit down, and sit up straight. Although this interaction was not always completely realized linguistically in ways the deaf children could understand (e.g., there was a great deal of dramatic stage whispering, which was rarely signed and never interpreted), Tom, Robbie, and Paul engaged in the competition.

For example, on a miserable winter day at the end of a rainy day recess, Mrs. Rogers announced "OK, our clay goes back," indicating the end of recess. This was not interpreted. Mrs. Rogers initiated the transition from recess to instruction time without notifying Mrs. Hart, who was still in the back of the room where she had spent the recess time visiting with students and admiring artwork. Mrs. Hart did not hear the announcement.

Suddenly there was much movement in the room, which Tom caught out of the corner of his eye. He looked around, puzzled, looked up at the clock and at his classmates moving about the room putting away their recess materials and returning to their seats. The thrill of competition reigned. Mrs. Hart also noted the movement and flashed the lights in the room. As soon as the lights flashed, Tom got up and carefully took his clay figure to the front table for storage.

The hearing children screeched and hissed, urging their classmates to hurry and sit down so they could earn the points. Tom was at the front table with his back to the room. A child cried out, "Hurry, Tom, hurry. *Tom*, Tom. Hurry, Tom." Another child from his row rushed to Tom, grabbed him and motioned him toward his chair. Both boys ran the few feet to their chairs, arms flailing. Tom slid into his chair and placed his arms on the table, twiddling his thumbs and looking forward. As soon as he sat down, Alicia, a hearing girl seated to his left, tapped him repeatedly on the shoulder. When he looked at her, she turned a steely gaze to her own folded hands, which were still. She hissed, "Tom, hold your hands." (This was not interpreted, nor could it possibly have been). He twiddled his thumbs a couple seconds longer and stopped. He adopted the model posture, holding very still with straight back, hands clasped on the desk, fingers unmoving, and eyes looking straight ahead. (Some of the children even tried to stop breathing and blinking their eyes during this moment of inspection.) After several seconds of stillness, Tom resumed twiddling.

At this moment Mrs. Hart was again in the front of the room, her official space for interpreting for the teacher. Tom smiled and signed GOOD. (It was not clear if he had an interlocutor or if he was commenting to himself. He could have been addressing this to Mrs. Hart.) Tom turned and smiled at his table mates. Mrs. Rogers made a serious face and looked for a quiet row. She announced, with the interpreter now signing what she said, that "it was close," but row one was the quiet row. This was not Tom's row. Alicia looked around with a scowl on her face, and another girl glared at Tom and Alicia. Someone in the row hissed "*You guys.*" Tom smiled, wiggled his shoulders, and looked across the room toward Paul and Robbie, who were seated in the triumphant row one.

It is clear from this scene that Tom's hearing classmates made some concessions to his deafness—touching him to get his attention, for example. Yet, as often tends to happen in settings strongly defined as "hearing contexts" (Erting 1982), when excitement escalated, Tom's classmates interacted with him as if he could choose to hear.

On another day a hearing classmate who could not sign tried another technique to provide covert help for his deaf neighbor. Mrs. Rogers had passed out the first page of an arithmetic quiz, and the students began calculating. Both Paul and Robbie rapidly finished the page. Each boy turned his paper over and started to draw on the blank back. Sally and Jerry, their hearing tablemates, both stared in horror at Paul's drawing, as Mrs. Rogers announced that the children should turn the first page over and leave it on the corner of their desks to signal that they have finished. She added ominously, "We won't draw on the backs." Paul was looking down, drawing, and did not see the interpreter when Mrs. Rogers' important but indirect directive was made. Jerry waved his hand to get Paul's attention and made a sweeping gesture with his hand on his paper, mouthing "erase." Paul looked around, then erased his drawings. Again, the hearing children acted on their understanding of the deaf children's lack of hearing as well as from the core of the "child collective" (Dyson 1989) that arises among students in classrooms.

Because deaf children were mainstreamed beginning in kindergarten, some of the hearing children had been in their mainstreaming class for three years. About once a year someone from the hearing impaired program taught a short sign language class for the hearing children. Some of the hearing second-graders could fingerspell and had command of a small lexicon of signs; they used both skills when initiating communication with the deaf children. However, the hearing children did not have systematic command of any kind of signing. Knowing fingerspelling and a few signs to add to their nonsigning methods of making contact with the deaf children still did not provide enough linguistic raw material to accomplish much interaction. Nonetheless, at Aspen School most of the adults were highly sentimental about children and language. Several teachers told me that once the hearing children had command of a few basic signs (an unspecified level of competence), they would be able to communicate with the deaf children. Unfortunately, none of the hearing children could sign fluently, and attempts at communication through language among the peers was often mangled and abrupt. The deaf and hearing children had virtually no linguistic resources for playing or joking together, for conversing about math, science, or social studies topics, or for building friendships.

SIGNING IN THE MAINSTREAM CLASSROOM

The hearing children's signing in the mainstreaming classroom fell into two categories: It was either completely incomprehensible and apparently confusing to the deaf children or it seemed to be understandable to the deaf children but (to an observer) impoverished. In the latter category, the signed utterances directed to the deaf children came from a very limited functional repertoire—directives and evaluations—which I termed *caretaker* talk.

Unintelligible Signing

Unintelligible communication was often directed at the deaf children in the mainstreaming classroom. One day, during the discussion following a movie about making wise purchases, the class discussed the ways people spend their money. Mrs. Rogers introduced the contrast between things people want and things people need. In the course of the discussion, they mentioned some household appliances (in the category of "things people need") that people spend money on, including washing machines. Peter, a hearing boy seated near Tom, noticed the way Mrs. Hart signed WASHING MACHINE and slowly copied the sign to himself. He practiced forming the sign many times, then he poked Tom, who turned around to look at him. Laboriously, Peter signed to Tom WASHING MACHINE. Tom stared blankly at Peter. By now this sign was far out of context since the class had moved on to another topic.

Tom provided a clue to his attitude toward the kind of hearing interactional behavior that Peter displayed. One day, as she was rushing out of the room with a very ill Paul, Mrs. Hart admonished Tom and Robbie to behave themselves in her absence. Tom responded, "They bother me," referring to the hearing children seated around him. Mrs. Hart answered, "You know what to do. Ignore them." Given that peer interaction is, in theory, a potential positive force in development, the pertinent theoretical question here is the extent to which children like Tom can withstand the bothersome and confusing forces of this kind of peer interaction. In fact, it was possible that Mrs. Hart was providing a deaf cultural solution for Tom to employ when confronted with hearing people whose odd use of signs resulted in interactional "bothering." If ignoring them seemed to be the best solution the deaf children could adopt, then one more avenue to the assimilation of deaf with hearing children was effectively barricaded.

Directives and Hints

During instruction, art, recess, and transitions, there were times when the hearing children used their sparse sign vocabularies to give the deaf students hints about what to do or, a bit more brusquely, to tell them what to do. At times the hearing children attempted to be helpful. One day, Mrs. Hart sent Tom back to Mrs. Rogers' room from the playground. He had to spend his recess finishing his thank-you letter to a troupe of jugglers who had visited and performed at the school. Mrs. Rogers was in the room, as were a few students who were also still working on their letters and drawings. The teacher went to Tom and said (with her voice only) "Draw a picture" and pointed to his paper. Tom stared at her. As Mrs. Rogers walked away, Janna looked at him and signed CRAYON (a sign the kids used to mean "color with crayons" or "color with a felt marking pen"). Tom signed back to her COLOR, COLOR, COLOR? Janna stared at him and after a pause (perhaps to try to comprehend the signs) nodded her head. Tom picked up a marker and started drawing.

Another day, the second-graders were working alone at their desks on their calendar worksheets. The task involved, for example, counting and recording the total number of Wednesdays in March. Tom was looking around the room, not working on his paper. Janna looked at him and signed COUNT. Tom signed back impatiently I KNOW-IT and turned away from Janna, pointedly avoiding eye contact with her. She scowled at him, and when Tom looked up to scan the room, looking for Mrs. Hart, Janna signed very slowly YOU ALONE (i.e., "You have to do the work by yourself"). Tom again averted his glance. Janna signed slowly REQUEST HELP. By this time both Peter and Janna were staring at Tom. Janna again signed REQUEST HELP.

Having noticed this exchange by now, Mrs. Rogers approached the table and began speaking to Tom. Mrs. Hart was not available because she was with Paul, still explaining Mrs. Rogers' instructions to him although Mrs. Rogers had moved over to Tom. Although she was speaking to him, Tom raised his hand and scanned the room once again and caught Mrs. Hart's attention. As soon as Mrs. Hart left Paul and joined Tom, Mrs. Rogers left her alone to explain the task.

About a week later, Janna had a new seat—next to Paul—facing the front of the class. The children were doing seatwork, and Mrs. Hart and Mrs. Rogers were roaming around the room. Janna poked Paul and showed him the spider-shaped ring she was wearing. Although Mrs. Rogers did not see Janna get Paul's attention, she did notice that Paul suspended work on his math paper to admire Janna's ring. She called out, "Janna, please touch Paul." (This was a method she had developed for enlisting the hearing children's help in physically managing the deaf children's attention.) Janna poked Paul and brusquely signed PAY ATTENTION, a much more explicit directive than Mrs. Rogers' tone of voice indicated.

Misplaced faith in the basic, that is, limited, lexicon of isolated signs emerged here again. Although they reflected Aspen School's open-hearted acceptance of the deaf children, the hearing child "signers" had very little knowledge of ways to engage in peer discourse with the deaf children. Although hearing children were certainly rude or gruff with each other from time to time, they had a larger pragmatic repertoire from which to select when they wanted to interact with hearing peers. When Janna tried to interact with her deaf peers, she had relatively few choices and, like the other hearing child signers, virtually always resorted to the most directive, least "polite," discourse forms.

Evaluations

The hearing children also frequently used the few signs they knew to evaluate or comment on the deaf children's work. Although these could be positive as well as negative comments, there was again a limited set of pragmatic choices available to the hearing children. During another rainy day recess, the children were working with clay at their desks. Robbie and Paul exhibited their clay figures to each other, risking violation of the recess rule ("stay in your seat") so they could be near someone who signed. Tom stayed at his table and worked intently on an intricate clay creation. His tablemates, Donald and Peter, were giggling and pointing to the clay form that Tom was fashioning. Janna, who was sitting across from Tom, signed GOOD to him, without trying to get his attention or make eye contact first.

Children's evaluations of each other are not particularly surprising instances of peer interaction. First, it is certainly true that children are interested in each other and express their interest in varied ways that are not always friendly or well mannered from an adult point of view. Second, Dyson (1989) identifies a feature of classroom life she calls the "child collective," a sense of being together at school that children express through collective action, group memory, group responses to school business (e.g., a substitute teacher), and concern over common problems and worries about the world. I would argue that the helping, managing, and evaluating that the hearing children directed toward the deaf children grew out of the social and moral order that structures such children's collectives.

The child collective that existed in Mrs. Rogers' classroom when the deaf children were there did not appear to result in, or even promote, assimilation among deaf and hearing children. Although there was a collective among the deaf second-grade boys (including Paul, Robbie, and Tom, and perhaps their hard of hearing classmate Lawrence, who was a new signer), the powerful social life that a class of children can build through talk and activity did not exist for the deaf second-graders in the mainstreaming classroom.

The deaf children were not only receivers of peer talk in the main-streaming classroom. There was evidence that they had identified a convenient and instrumental use for communication with the hearing children. However, just as the functions of communication from hearing to deaf children were limited, so the deaf children limited the communication they addressed to the hearing students. Almost exclusively, when the deaf children signed to the hearing students, they enlisted heuristic functions. They sought information and asked questions, and they looked for clarification of aspects of classroom business. For personal functions, that is, for making contact with others or for expressing opinions, the deaf boys often looked all the way across the room and signed to their deaf classmates or walked across the room to hold signed conversations.

Late one afternoon, the youngsters were finishing their math papers when Robbie remembered the play equipment from recess. He attracted Paul's attention and signed to him over the heads of the hearing children, WHERE THAT BALL? WHERE THAT BALL? Paul shrugged. Robbie then signed to Roland, a hearing boy at their table, WHERE THAT BALL? Roland stared at him but did not respond. Robbie tried again and signed and mouthed BALL, BALL. There was still no response from Roland, who continued to stare wide-eyed at Robbie, who abandoned his attempt to locate the ball.

During another indoor recess, Tom took a break for a drink of water, then went back to his desk to finish his seatwork. He stood up and hopped on one leg at his desk while he worked on the math problems. When he finished, he tapped Janna twice. She ignored him, so he pulled on her shoulder to make her turn around. He slowly signed to her FINISH THIS (index and eyegaze to paper on his desk) PLAY? (i.e., "When this is finished, is it playtime?")

Janna looked at Tom, paused, and shook her head as he signed FINISH. After he signed PLAY, she slowly signed PLAY YES and turned away from Tom to the group of kids at her desk (Roland, Peter, and Donald). Here, Tom was seeking information about the business at hand: retrieving part of his recess time. The only person at hand to ask was Janna, so he attempted to get the information from her. Although she did not grasp his question at first, she seemed to figure out what he was trying to say when she responded.

Although the hearing students seemed to like the deaf students and had never demonstrated any overt lack of respect or explicit cruelty toward their deaf classmates, communication between the two groups of children was constrained. These observations suggest that a great gap exists between the idealized assumptions that bolster placement policies in local public school programs for deaf children and their realization in deaf children's lives at school. A closer look at real children who are students in a very typical kind of mainstreaming program where some of their hearing agemates even know some signs indicates that the ideal is still far from our reach.

The deaf and hearing children were physically integrated with each other in the mainstreaming classroom. With access to linguistic and interactional resources, perhaps they would have communicated and expanded their limited pragmatic patterns of interacting through language. However, the functional patterns found in the two groups' interactions through language were clear and undeniably limited. At times these children who did not share a language negotiated at the boundary that separated them, but they did not have the resources actually to cross it.

Within a Vygotskyan theoretical framework about the path toward literacy and other higher functions, the interaction described here is impoverished. It not only fails to promote development but possibly holds it back. Many teachers have seen marginalized children who appear simply to abandon efforts to engage with school. It is possible that deaf children's struggles to communicate with nonsigning hearing people simply reinforce their suspicion that it is fruitless to even make the effort to communicate and engage with others. It does not seem likely that these interactions could lead to a future world where Deaf people and nonsigning hearing people easily assimilate.

However, to bolster the point that the children were interested in each other (and perhaps that human beings in groups are compelled to forge bonds of some kind), the children did make contact with each other in nonlinguistic ways. In fact, nonlanguage contact was the vehicle by which both personal and interactional functions were attempted between the two groups of children.

For example, during a math lesson, the second-graders were learning to tell time. After Mrs. Rogers worked through many examples with the class, they began a worksheet on the topic. Jason, a hearing tablemate of

Paul's and Robbie's complained aloud about being bored with clocks and telling time, and he did not turn to his worksheet as Robbie and Paul did. Hence he was unoccupied when Robbie and Paul finished their own work while many other children were still working. Robbie began squirming in his chair, unwittingly making a loud squeaking noise. As he danced in his seat, he turned to Jason, and they traded amusing facial expressions. Paul finished his worksheet, got Jason's attention, and proceeded to make funny faces and use his pencil as if it were a gear shift. Soon, Mrs. Rogers visited their table to check their worksheets, and the peer contact stopped.

The next day during math, Tom unsuccessfully tried to make contact with Peter (his hearing seat mate). Tom began by looking at Peter, then at his own math paper. He glanced again at Peter, back at his own paper, then shook his head, and shrugged his shoulders. Tom made a tiny sign, WHAT? although it was not clear whether he addressed this to Peter or to himself. Twice more he turned to Peter, each time shaking his head and moving his eyegaze to his own paper. Peter never responded. However, Mrs. Hart, at the front of the room interpreting for Mrs. Rogers' instructional talk, noted Tom's activity and glared at him. Tom immediately returned his gaze to Mrs. Hart and adopted the posture that signaled "paying attention."

For the purposes of learning and development, the interaction among deaf and hearing children in the mainstreaming classroom as it was configured at Aspen School was highly constrained and not developmentally helpful. In addition, the generative social power of a phenomenon like the child collective was not available to the deaf children for serving their immediate, everyday social needs. Mrs. Rogers was correct, however, when she commented that the deaf and hearing children did not appear to be mean or rude to each other. In fact, there were nonlinguistic patterns of interaction that led to personal contact among the children. However, few parents of hearing children would judge sufficient for their own children the personal contact and peer interaction that was available in the mainstream for the deaf second-graders at Aspen School.

Chapter 6

The Self-Contained Classroom

at Aspen School

The contrast between Robbie, Paul, and Tom's mainstreaming class-room and the self-contained classroom for deaf and hard of hearing children was striking. The most obvious dissimilarities were the physical arrangement and the people in the room. Mrs. Rogers arranged the mainstreaming room so that children sat in neat rows of tables, where each student occupied an assigned seat. In contrast, Ms. Roberts and Ms. Adams arranged the self-contained classroom into "centers," where different kinds of activities took place. The children sat at tables or on rugs and moved among the areas of the room, but they were not assigned individual desks. Rather, they had individual storage cabinets (called cubbies) where they kept their lunchboxes, bookbags, caps, and jackets during the day, and each student had a folder for school work. Books and materials needed for each area were stored on nearby shelves. In addition, there were at most thirteen children in the self-contained classroom, and often five to six adults (Ms. Roberts, Ms. Adams, various interpreters, instructional assistants, and specialists). This was not a setting conducive to the teacher-centered order of the mainstreaming classroom. Indeed, the teachers organized their space, time, and human resources intentionally to create a setting where the deaf children would be able to interact through language with peers and with adults. Students often worked with close adult guidance, but adults rarely exercised complete control of interaction, as Mrs. Rogers tried to do. It is not surprising that Tom, Robbie, and Paul (as well as most of their deaf and hard of hearing classmates) preferred the self-contained classroom, where they had more flexibility, a great deal more autonomy, and many more conversational partners.

Another important, although not surprising, difference is that Ms. Roberts's and Ms. Adams's descriptions of their classroom and their teaching also reflected a distinct approach to teaching deaf children. They had made a professional choice to pursue training in this area early in their careers and were very knowledgeable about the education of deaf children. In addition, both were interested in children and their development and had devoted time to learning about teaching and learning in general. They each had a solid understanding of pedagogy as well as of teaching deaf children, and as a result, they were the most unconventional (and arguably the best trained) of the six teachers of the deaf at Aspen School. The two reported that they were regarded as radical by more conventional teachers of the deaf at neighboring school districts. In the late 1980s the idea that deaf children might be regarded as ASL/English bilinguals (or potentially so) had not reached their district, although bilingual-bicultural programs in residential schools in Indiana and California had received a certain amount of publicity by that time. Most of their colleagues in other districts held a traditional view of their students as impaired children who required rehabilitation. As in most states, neighboring public school programs were Total Communication programs, where teachers spoke English and signed a manual code for English as the medium of instruction.

Their deaf education training, their signing ability, and their small class gave Ms. Roberts and Ms. Adams a clear advantage over Mrs. Rogers in working with the deaf students. Obviously teachers of the deaf and general education mainstreaming teachers cannot be expected to have the same knowledge about deaf children. In addition, where Mrs. Rogers constantly felt that she had to make sure her classroom was an equal placement for the deaf children, an almost impossible task under the circumstances, the two teachers of the deaf did not have this concern. Their classroom existed on its own terms, and they did not have to develop a notion of their room as an altered version of a regular classroom, rearranged to integrate a group of different children. All of the children in their classroom were "different," and they had the inclination, the training, and the duty to confront these disparities and devise ways to teach the children.

Ms. Roberts and Ms. Adams did not puzzle over how to achieve equal educational opportunity at Aspen School through manipulations of placement. Both simply believed that it was not possible. They did not believe that teachers could begin from a model of schooling for hearing children and then make a few additions and other changes in order to create schooling for deaf children. Rather, they believed that specific assumptions underlay schooling for deaf children and that it had to be seen as schooling specially designed to address deaf children's critical language and communication needs along with the canon of elementary school knowledge. As Ms. Roberts suggested, adding a sign language interpreter to a class with a "hearing format" did not constitute education for deaf children, even though it appeared to satisfy the requirements for a placement in the least restrictive environment. And Ms. Adams, who was more optimistic about mainstreaming than Ms. Roberts, still realized that it was not particularly useful for the deaf students' learning at Aspen School.

Unlike Mrs. Rogers' room, there was a great deal of observable activity in the self-contained classroom. In particular, the children were engaged in school tasks and in conversation and interaction a great deal of the time. Ms. Adams and Ms. Roberts were able to design a classroom specifically to respond to deaf children's learning needs, as they and the children's parents saw them. Not only was there more activity in the self-contained classroom, but the teachers also used ASL much of the time. Features of the self-contained classroom suggested that it could function as a context for learning. Since the deaf children could participate fully in all the activities in this setting, they were busier, more engaged, more conversational, and more argumentative than they could be in the mainstreaming classroom, and they were able to employ a wide range of language uses. Just as language was one of the troublesome features that kept the mainstreaming classroom from being a context for learning, language and its use were the key features that promoted the self-contained classroom as a context for learning.

Having decided to use ASL as the medium of instruction for signing deaf students several years earlier, Ms. Roberts had engineered the hiring of Mrs. Hart. Ms. Adams sought a teaching position at Aspen School in part because the use of ASL as a medium of instruction was compatible with her own views about educating deaf children. A group of native signers all claimed independently that the three adults, as well as Tom, Robbie, and Paul, were signing ASL. It was clear that social and symbolic life in the deaf classroom was structured by adults who knew ASL. As a result, classroom activities were intelligible to the deaf students, and they could engage in the social and symbolic life they afforded in multiple ways as their ASL competence grew.

In contrast to the mainstreaming classroom, in the self-contained classroom the teachers believed that deaf children could and should actually participate in all activities. Further, in order to learn they had to assume many roles beyond that of the relatively passive receiver role foisted on them in the mainstreaming classroom. Several patterns of language use grew from the fact that Ms. Roberts, Ms. Adams, and Mrs. Hart conceived of the self-contained room as a class for signing deaf children (as opposed to a speech-based class for hearing children with an interpreter). Accordingly, the adults purposefully used language to structure activities that the deaf children could participate in and comprehend. Importantly, in this context the boys could regard language and print as objects, that is, they could develop metalinguistic reflectiveness about both English and ASL. In addition, they had many opportunities to employ language as a tool: They learned to exploit the mediational possibilities of their more dominant language, ASL, to crack the code of English.

Much of the instructional energy in the self-contained classroom was built around communication and use of language both face-to-face and in print. Three recurring activities—journal writing, book sharing, and language lessons—constituted the core of the language curriculum for the deaf children and provided abundant opportunities for the students to wrestle with their languages. Instruction took place in small groups. The teachers preferred to teach the boys in sequences of intensive one-to-one conversation between one of the adults and one of the children. Group conversations were not discouraged, but often adults were responding to a child's specific questions while the others continued with their tasks or worked with another adult. The organization of each activity was well known to the children and somewhat flexible, but adults organized the key portions of the activities: when the books were shared and read, when the content of the language lesson was presented, or when the journal topics were selected and approved.

Tom, Robbie, and Paul had reputations as "talkers" (not literally speakers of oral English but rather as social operators), which had developed over the years the teachers had known them. The teachers' characterizations were accurate and reflected in the boys' conversational behavior. The most talkative, Robbie preferred to initiate conversations, and during lessons he virtually never participated in a conversation that was not related to the lesson or the work they were doing. Tom was regarded as less talkative than Robbie. The quality of Tom's interaction contributed to his personal claim to fame: his imaginative and creative storytelling. He was also, however, easily distracted and often tried to engage peers in conversations that ranged far from school topics. Tom, in turn, was regarded as more talkative and outgoing than Paul, who was perceived as the quietest and most self-reliant of the three. Although Paul was the newest signer of the three, he possessed sophisticated and assertive disputing skills. He was the only one among them who had learned to specify the nature of his complaints when the other two tried to converse with him excessively when Paul was "working." His habit was to state very clearly, "Stop bothering me" or "Stop interrupting me."

Despite their individual differences, over the range of activities in the self-contained classroom, Tom, Robbie, and Paul demonstrated a preference for each other as conversational partners. Indeed, they took intentional actions to seek out people with whom they could easily communicate in a language they had in common and about topics they shared an interest in, just as they avoided nonsigners. Preferring not to interact at school with people who could not sign, they routinely declined to engage or even to sit with nonsigning substitute teachers, instructional aides, and other staff who attempted to enter the social life of the deaf classroom. When Robbie had to work with a nonsigning person in class, he lost his charm completely and became a very difficult boy to get along with.

PATTERNS OF LANGUAGE USE IN LITERACY ACTIVITIES

Many activities in the self-contained classroom were generated by Ms. Roberts's beliefs about how children learn language, the best ways to foster early literacy, and the kinds of activities that best give deaf children access to language. She believed that the foundation of literacy for her deaf students was the ability to move smoothly between ASL and English. The primary benefit of journal time, then, was to practice putting thoughts and ideas into pictures and words, to perform word-level translations between signs and English words, and simply to "play with language," as Ms. Roberts described it. She knew that play, a key element of learning, was missing in most of her students' lives out of school. Journal time provided a period when the students could engage with symbols (face-to-face language, drawing, and printed words) to make stories and art and to share information and narratives.

Formal English instruction was incorporated into another activity, "language," during which the adults engaged the children in intentional tutoring in English, again primarily at the word and morpheme levels. The second graders did not study sentence construction formally, although brief exercises involving sentences occurred during journal time or when a paragraph or story was ready for its final edit. The emphasis in the second-graders' language lessons was on vocabulary. Instructional conversations most often took place through ASL, and the hearing teachers signed without speaking English. As with journal writing and most other instruction in the deaf classroom, teaching took place during one-to-one conversations between an adult and a child in response to the specific task the child was working on and the adult's sense of the child's needs.

The main function of adult-initiated conversations was testing, where teachers drew out a child on a feature of the task or a topic chosen by the adult. The adults' routine was to assess the children's learning and to encourage broader perspectives by asking them to elaborate, to give definitions and examples, or to discuss the topics. These moments of teaching were frequent and brief. During one 43-minute-long journal writing event, for example, 122 one-to-one instructional conversations took place among three adults and five children. In another 75-minute-long language lesson approximately 140 one-to-one conversations took place between two adults and five children. For several weeks in October, the boys worked on learning an inventory of lexical items termed "feeling words" (e.g., *surprised, worried, frightened, proud*). As the children drew faces expressing emotions and labeled their drawings with printed words they copied from a master list, the adults answered the children's questions (of which there were few) and initiated conversations with each child in turn.

As an example, during one such conversation, Ms. Adams sat down next to Paul and began by asking him to "tell me what it means," pointing to the labels on his drawings. Under a picture of a scared-looking face Paul carefully printed the word *scared*. Although it was clear from his drawing that Paul understood what *scared* means, he had some trouble with Ms. Adams's request to provide a definition. She provided the first response herself, by telling a short story about a scary event. After this example, Paul was able to adequately demonstrate what he knew by answering Ms. Adams's questions about being scared. He employed her model and defined through description. He offered an inventory of frightening events: suddenly being plunged into darkness in an old house and meeting up with a monster. Paul's problem was not so much providing a definition of *scared* as it was knowing what *meaning* consisted of. His was not so much a language competence problem as it was a more typical instance of a young student trying to figure out what the teacher wants to hear. After Ms. Adams engaged him and gave him a model to use for the definition task, he accomplished it by himself. In subsequent conversations he defined *happy, proud,* and *sad.*

These teaching interactions depended on the adults' ability to correctly predict the points at which they should intervene, to recognize strategies that did not work, and to provide support for strategies that did. Critically, successful interactions depended upon something very simple: mutual intelligibility, a language in common between teacher and child. The teaching conversations enabled the children to express their ideas, to demonstrate their knowledge, and to make practical use of text to gather new information. These essential learning activities were simply unavailable in the mainstreaming classroom.

For the participants, book sharing served several compatible purposes that encouraged conscious exploration of translating relationships between ASL and printed English as well as between Deaf people and their languages. From the adults' point of view, the purpose of this activity was to give the children opportunities to make contact with real children's books (as opposed to basal readers) and to use books and their contents as props and raw material for meaningful face-to-face communication in ASL or speech, drawing, and writing in English. Interwoven with this was a serious social and cultural purpose. Mrs. Hart was especially involved in this activity, partly because she valued time spent with the children. Many times she referred to the strong bond she felt with them because they were deaf. She also assumed a responsibility for making their lives at school—and their views of themselves as valuable, capable human beings—more positive than her own had been. Mrs. Hart also valued the opportunity to use ASL for direct interaction with the children. For her, an event like story reading, in contrast to events where she was the sign language interpreter, presented an uninterrupted block of time during which she could organize her interaction with the students, generate and express her thoughts, and use her preferred mode of interaction to communicate with them directly.

Book sharing was a very pleasant event in the self-contained class. Discussing books and watching the performance of stories were ideal moments for informal interaction framed by narratives. Stories, of course, provide a stage for dramatic, virtually theatrical, ASL. Although they were beginning readers, the children knew very well that books were dependable repositories of stories. In addition, during free reading time, the boys routinely used books as social resources for information, facts, and evidence that came in handy during disputes. As many children do, the boys threw around their intellectual weight by citing facts about dinosaurs, fingerspelling the names of many kinds of sharks, or bolstering their claims with the authority of a book, all in order to gain social ground or win arguments.

The adults did not use book reading solely to entertain the students but also to teach them about the world, using a mix of symbolic media. For example, when Mrs. Hart shared a book about Johnny Appleseed with the children, she kept a map handy and tied Johnny's travels to United States geography and the country, state, and cities the children had visited, where they lived, and where their school was located. In order to participate they had to pay careful attention to both Mrs. Hart and to the print on the map. When the children commented on Johnny's lack of shoes in illustrations, she discussed poverty in general terms, explaining how hard it sometimes is for many people to earn enough money to buy the things they need.

During book reading Mrs. Hart adopted a pace that differed markedly from the hearing teachers' methods of book reading with hearing children. Her pattern of storytelling was to rapidly and silently read the print to herself (holding the book so that only she could see it), then to translate the meaning into ASL. Only after she signed that portion of the story did she hold the book down to show the pages to the children, discuss it, and respond to their comments about it. This resulted in constant, deliberately timed movement between the illustrations and the text. Out of the fifty-four-minute book reading/sharing episode about Johnny Appleseed, Mrs. Hart actually used the book for only fourteen minutes. From the telling of the story, communication flowed between discussions about it and expansions and elaborations that grew from the illustrations and from Mrs. Hart's rendition of the book.

For instance, the children looked closely at the print and the illustrations in attempts to locate and recount the story that Mrs. Hart had just related to them. Often they moved beyond the illustration and the text and made interpretations and personal responses. Tom, for example, claimed that he could identify Deaf people in book illustrations by choosing people whose hands were drawn so that they appeared to be signing or fingerspelling. As a group the boys also recounted fight scenes or other dramatic events depicted in illustrations and included themselves as characters.

Although both Ms. Adams and Ms. Roberts knew ASL and operated under the assumption that Deaf culture existed, they were not sure exactly which of its features (beyond use of ASL and visits from deaf adults) were pertinent to deaf education nor how it could contribute to their classroom. Like Mrs. Hart, Ms. Roberts and Ms. Adams felt it was important to guide the children's "visual attention." To this end, they all provided explicit directions about watching other signers and about being seen by others. However, the hearing teachers' methods of leading book sharing were very different from Mrs. Hart's. When Ms. Roberts led book sharing, she presented a large stack of books to show the children. The purpose of the activity from her viewpoint was not to read a book or to tell a story but to offer an array of books that the children could choose from at another time.

Although Ms. Roberts's stacks of books were impressive, the sheer number and the time available for showing them entailed very brief perusals and a rapid pace. She displayed many pages of some of the books and only a few pages or the cover of many of them. She tied her conversation to the content of books (the printed texts), to the children's memories of books on similar topics (e.g., sea life, airplanes, Alaska, and Navajo native legends), and to their familiarity with favorite books that regularly appeared in the classroom for intensive repeated readings. Hence, she was providing many possible connections between the books and the ongoing conversation. Although the activity was certainly enjoyable, the procedure for viewing the books was unpredictable and very rapid, and the children squirmed and let their attention wander. Since they had no reassurance that they would be able to take a good look at the pictures, there were unpleasant moments when they complained that they could not see and pushed each other out of the way.

Where Mrs. Hart made the telling of the story and the viewing of the pictures two distinct but related activities, Ms. Roberts used the very common strategy of combining them. During her many years of teaching hearing and deaf children in elementary settings, she had acquired the ability to read upside-down print. This valuable skill eases the burdens of book sharing for hearing teachers of hearing children. Yet, in Ms. Roberts's case, this procedure made her book sharing with the deaf children a highly difficult task for her and for the children. For her part, Ms. Roberts had to juggle the book on her lap, trying to maintain an angle of visibility for the children, while using both of her hands to sign. Looking at the text as she signed, she could not scan her audience to make enough regular eye contact with the children to hold the floor, a critical pragmatic skill in signed discourse. The children had to make on-line choices between two highly valued activities: watching signed translations of portions of books and viewing the pictures. In addition, the collapsing of two related story elements (the story and the pictures) into one lent the illusion that the children were actually "seeing" both the story and the pictures in the time it took for Ms. Roberts to sign the story. In reality, however, there was not enough time for the children to satisfy their wishes to see both the print and the illustrations because Ms. Roberts, like even very skilled hearing signers, chose a nearly impossible "hearing" interactional path for book reading with deaf children. Using procedures that work for hearing teacher-student interaction was difficult and less successful than exploiting the pragmatic strategies of deaf signers.

LANGUAGE AS A TOPIC OF CONVERSATION

With some exceptions, like "hearing book sharing," patterns of language use in the self-contained class did engage the deaf students in instruction. One outcome of this higher level of engagement was that the children and adults had access to many shared topics of conversation, among them language itself. For example, book sharing was always an opportunity for instructing the children about the importance of paying attention to other signers. Mrs. Hart offered specific direct advice as well as indirect tactics to help the children learn to engage in signed communication. She and the other adults routinely reminded the deaf children that they had to watch the person who was signing. As she told the story of Johnny Appleseed, she directed the children's attention by signing WATCH-ME immediately before she fingerspelled a word or name (e.g., Johnny Appleseed's name, J-O-H-N C-H-A-P-M-A-N) or stated a number (e.g., the year of Johnny Appleseed's birth, 1774). Naturally, the other half of this equation was reminding the children to look at the others to make sure they were watching before beginning a conversational turn.

Mrs. Hart also successfully used play to emphasize the importance of watching her signing. One of her playful, less direct tactics was to engage the children's attention by warning them that she was going to trick them. For example, she began the reading of a book about Johnny Appleseed by blandly announcing that Johnny Appleseed was famous for "feeding whales." When the children noisily disagreed with her, she asked "He fed sharks?" The children began giggling and responding with equally silly answers, but not all of them were paying attention. A moment later, when

Mrs. Hart picked up the book she calmly reported, "I have a book about whales." This time all the children shrieked with laughter and signed NO in disagreement. Mrs. Hart strategically used the first moments of book reading to make certain that the children were engaged in the activity.

During the book reading described earlier, Mrs. Hart devoted 18 out of a total 54 minutes to introducing the book and the activity. This briefing strategy was also related to paying attention. In her introduction she included an explicit description of her procedure for reading the story, reassuring the children that she understood their need to look at her signing as well as their desire to see the pictures. She explained that she would go through the text briefly and give them plenty of time to look at the pictures (she kept her promise). Finally, she announced that she would sign the story. Although she virtually always signed with the children, she still explicitly informed the children about how she would be communicating with them. In addition to naming her mode of delivery ("signing"), her specification made clear to the children her commitment to engage with them.

Mrs. Hart exhibited another pattern that resulted in making sign language, fingerspelling, and English explicit objects of attention. She commented on fingerspelling etiquette and proper and improper signing. For example, at the beginning of the book reading, after she fingerspelled his name, she invented a name sign for Johnny Appleseed. But she made the interesting comment that this was not his real name sign, just one she made up to use for now. She cautioned that it was not respectful to just make up name signs for people, that politeness required that you spell people's names. Interestingly, when Mrs. Hart told the story, she neither used her invented sign name nor spelled his whole name. She consistently referred to him as John, fingerspelling J-O-H-N every time he was named in text. Apparently her own stated rules in favor of fingerspelling proper names and against ad hoc signs organized her book-reading behavior.

In the self-contained classroom, several less-than-conventional signs were used by children and teachers as part of their shared schoolroom code, for example, ʟUNCH and ʀECESS. These code-signs were members of a category of illegitimate signs, which Mrs. Hart was careful to distinguish from ASL. She did not hesitate to correct the signing children and adults in the classroom if they used a sign she considered improper ASL. Although it was not always possible to predict which signs she would consider improper, she was like many deaf ASL signers in disapproving of signs that seemed to be "invented by hearing people," were obviously and peculiarly initialized (KIND or REAL), or encoded English morphemes that ASL does not have (third person pronouns, e.g., HE or SHE, and grammatical and derivational inflections, e.g., -LY, -ING, -S).

In addition to engaging the deaf children in conversations about communication and signing, Ms. Roberts, Ms. Adams, and Mrs. Hart maintained a context where the children could exercise their curiosity about writing systems and languages and how they work. Accordingly, Tom, Robbie, and Paul were beginning to develop reflectiveness about language, how it could be used, and how various people used it, a capacity that is critical for developing literacy (e.g., Dyson 1989, 1991). Although the primary languages (as media of interaction and as topics of conversation) in the self-contained classroom were ASL and English (primarily in print), other languages entered the discourse from time to time. During book sharing one day, the boys looked through a book about children from all over the world. One page featured photographs of a girl from India demonstrating handshapes that accompanied a dance. Since the boys assumed that she was signing, these photographs captured their attention. They began asking the teachers about the girl's signing. Paul asked Ms. Roberts if that kind of signing was hard for the girl to learn. Tom wanted to know what the signs meant. Ms. Roberts explained that it was not precisely signing but rather gestures that showed meaning in the dance; for example, one of them represented *fish*. She also explained that the girl learned those movements from other dancers and that she perfected them by practice, just like any of us develops a skill.

On another day, during a unit about Guatemala, Ms. Roberts showed the boys photographs of Mayan writing and some line drawings of the symbols. She explained about the destruction of the great Mayan libraries and the loss of the collections of books during the expansion of Spain to the New World. She emphasized that the pictured examples of Mayan writing were ancient and that people now did not know exactly what the symbols meant, although they were trying to figure it out. She also described in detail the construction of Mayan books, which resulted in books that looked quite different from modern Western-style bound volumes.

Since the writings had been discovered at kings' tombs, the lesson was full of detail and a certain amount of gore. The children's interest was focused on the peculiar writing—the ancient Mayan symbols—and their meanings. They persisted in asking what the texts said and wanted someone to tell them the story of the dead kings. Ms. Roberts repeated the little that she knew, that the story was about a king who was called "Eighteen Rabbits," according to the symbols that had been deciphered. The children were unsatisfied and asked about the rest of the symbols and the story. Interestingly, they also wanted to know how the particular symbols in the king's name meant *eighteen* and *rabbits*. ("Where does it say *rabbit* and where does it say *eighteen?*" "What does *seventeen* look like?") When Ms. Roberts explained that she could not tell them since she could not read the Mayan writing, Tom did not believe her. He discussed this with Robbie and Paul and asked other adults in the room. They quickly determined that no one knew how to read Mayan writing even though everyone was purportedly a reader.

This amazing fact took on a life of its own among the children in the deaf and hard of hearing classroom. To be sure, the existence of such a writing system (and its violent history and tragic extinction) was intriguing in itself. But the fact that the adults in the room could not read it was almost beyond belief. This piece of news was passed underground among the children. Near the end of the school day, hours after the morning lesson on the Mayan writing system, the children were still gathering around the pictures, gossiping about the adults' failure to read the texts.

It is clear that the children's ability to carefully observe print and to express their deep curiosity about languages and writing was fostered by the general intelligibility of interaction in the deaf classroom and by the children's opportunities to participate in it. Since the children were able to use language to gain broad general knowledge, they were aware of the existence of other languages in the world. They knew, for example, that Ms. Roberts spoke and wrote Spanish. In addition, although the children lived far from any non-English-speaking nation, they had Hispanic and Filipino classmates who came from bilingual homes. Finally, some of the children had lived in Europe (primarily in the West Germany of the time) when their fathers or mothers were posted abroad with the military. Their curiosity about languages resulted in an eye for detail that was sometimes surprising.

During a slide show about Guatemala, Tom noticed a red stop sign in one of the slides. The word *alto* was printed on the sign in large white letters. Although the room was dark, he leaped up from the floor where he was sitting, pointed to the screen, and signed (in the light from the slide projector) WHERE S-T? WHERE S-T? He expected a stop sign to display the letter combination *st* and demanded an explanation of their absence. Ms. Roberts responded in terms of languages in general (Guatemala uses

Spanish on signs) and in terms of symbolic equivalences (the word in Spanish for *stop* is *alto*). A question about such a small symbolic detail is not generally expected from deaf children, especially when being deaf is equated with pathology. However, this is exactly the type of question that many young children, who seem compelled to seek symbols and puzzle over symbolic codes, could be expected to ask.

Explicit communication about language and writing also emerged in journal writing, when the children initiated conversations about writing by asking questions. The boys' questions were indicative of their approach to print and their budding strategies for tackling the relation between two important symbol systems. They were especially interested in finding the right word or words to translate their signs into English. For example, to spell a word like *turtle*, they might ask any nearby signing adult, or Robbie—who was known as a good informant about many words—or look in a dictionary. However, one day Tom wanted to write about a turtle "leaping through the air and biting a man on the nose; it starts with *t*." He was insistent that the word he was looking for was not *turtle*, which he already knew how to write. He was looking for another word with *t*. Finally, one of the third-graders recognized that the *t* Tom was explicitly naming was the *t* in *teenage*, not the *t* in *turtle*, and that he wanted to write "Teenage Mutant Ninja Turtle." The boys' energy during writing was devoted to gathering collections of words to adequately express their ideas and to spelling them correctly. In order to gather the words they needed to fill out their English texts, they used a great deal of representational and personal language to narrate, interpret, and comment on their stories. Although they did not always agree on what kind of matches were needed, they were single-minded in their searches for written English words to match their ASL utterances. The three boys argued at length one day about creating a name sign for "Little Red Riding Hood." Although Tom and Paul proposed calling her RED, using an uninitialized ASL lexical item, Robbie argued long and hard that her name sign had to include an R handshape borrowed from fingerspelling to adequately represent her name. (Tom and Paul ended up accepting Robbie's idea.) Although the boys' interactional world was structured by signing and ASL and not by English, their access to a shared language provided an avenue for making English—and representations of English words in spelling and writing—a topic of conversation.

All three adults fostered the search for collections of equivalents in the two languages by clearly marking distinctions between ASL and English.

This in itself is an important difference. Anecdotal evidence from highly literate deaf adults, for whom print English serves a wide range of functions, suggests that early awareness that signing and print constitute different languages contributed to their achievement of literacy (Ramsey 1984). Yet in educational settings, distinctions between ASL and English have gone unmarked since ASL was an unrecognized phenomenon until recent decades and is still regarded by many teachers as unimportant or even a hindrance to deaf children's learning. Over the history of deaf education, language was often interpreted by both teachers and deaf students to mean only correct English sentences, not signing.

In the self-contained classroom, the adults' messages about this important difference went beyond simply marking it. All three adults struggled to make the rules of English spelling and syntax explicit and reasonable to the children. Mrs. Hart sometimes announced to the children that "English is weird," that is, irregular and difficult to explain. In fact, this motto was often uttered in the classroom by the children as well. In addition, all three adults also told the children explicitly that it was important for them to learn to spell and write English correctly and that this task required attention to detail, searches for equivalents, constant movement between English and ASL, and a type of conscious and inflexible observation of rules that face-to-face conversation did not usually require.

One of the complications for the boys was that ASL/English equivalents were often seemingly unbalanced sets of words and signs. They were learning that to capture in print what they might perceive as one or two signs might require several English words. During reading, the opposite was true as well, when an English sentence might be translated into one morphologically complex ASL sign. In fact, one of the third-grade children in the self-contained classroom, David, had acquired such facility with this kind of translation that he could read "aloud" and make very rapid translations of English phrases and sentences into ASL signs, for example, "The bus swayed back and forth as it drove up the hill" and "The large kite got smaller and smaller as it went higher in the sky." David was demonstrating both his discovery of a translating relationship between ASL and English and the facility with which he could move between the two languages.

Mrs. Hart was especially insistent on correctness and diction and took pains to locate the exact English words to translate the children's signing into print, illustrated while helping Tom during journal writing one day. He had drawn a picture and was ready to write a story about it. Ms.

Adams and Ms. Roberts circulated among the journal writers, and Ms. Adams complimented Tom on his "nice gorilla" and offered to help him learn a new word, *gorilla*. With the temperament of an artist, Tom declined. He had been narrating the story of his picture to Mrs. Hart in fluent ASL as he plotted his drawing, and she knew that the drawing was really Bigfoot, a Sasquatch, a word she could approximate in speech but not spell. She asked the native English speakers in the room how to spell "Sasquatch," printed it out on a piece of paper, and gave it to Tom.

By her example, she demonstrated that there were specific English words that translated signs (or told stories) better than other English words, that it was permissible for an adult to ask others about words, and that the enterprise of locating and writing out these important words was worth doing, even on behalf of an eight-year-old deaf child. This event provided evidence of Mrs. Hart's respect for, and expectations for, the children's emerging English print literacy and also indicated the seriousness with which she approached the difficult task of writing English.

The hearing teachers also helped the children with spelling and translation. However, their teaching conversations during writing centered on and modeled composition processes, even though the children were focused not on composition but on drawing and labeling drawings first. Composing sentences was a second priority. The boys devoted time to producing their drawings, most of which illustrated a story that they spun out with peers as they shared materials and drew. Although they were serious about journal writing and exceedingly task oriented, their social energy was devoted to telling the stories that illustrated their drawings (i.e., representational language) and asking for specific information about written English words (i.e., heuristic functions). Hence, such issues as the elaboration of the written version of the text, the sequence and internal logic of information presented, and its segmentation into paragraphs were not their main concern.

The focus of Paul's interest during writing was on English words. During free time, he often stood at the board and wrote an inventory of all the words he knew how to write. At this point in his learning, individual words were extremely valuable objects to him, manifestations of the rapid accumulation of vocabulary he was experiencing in second grade. In mid-November, Paul decided to introduce a holiday theme into his journal book and drew a picture of Santa Claus. He drew with great concentration for twelve minutes and initiated only one conversation, with Robbie, to narrate his Santa story and make personal comments on his Christmas scene. As he began to write about his picture, he asked Ms. Roberts to tell him the date, a formula that always marked the initiation of writing during this period. (For marking the termination of writing, the boys wrote in large letters, on a separate line at the end of their texts, "the end.") As he wrote his Santa Claus entry, Paul interacted with adults heuristically, puzzling over a word, then seeking an adult's help with the equivalent.

In order to get help during writing, he used very subtle eye gaze shifts, to which the teachers in the self-contained classroom were highly sensitive. As he filled in a story about Santa Claus, Paul signed to himself T̲OY, marking his search for a specific written English lexical item by using a manual code for English (MCE) initialized sign. He gazed at Ms. Adams and signed T̲OY again, marking it as a question with the ASL WH-question nonmanual marker. She took this as a request and mouthed "toy" (without speaking aloud), fingerspelled "T-O-Y," then mouthed it again. Paul wrote a *t* on his paper and looked up again. Ms. Adams copied the sign he used, confirming that this was the equivalent he was seeking. He nodded his head, and she provided the next letter, *o*. Paul wrote "o," then guessed the next letter, R? S? Ms. Adams provided *y*, and Paul wrote "y."

Here, Paul was seeking an English word equivalent, a search that he marked with a specific initialized sign. He mediated his search by signing to himself, using the sign as a tool. In contrast, when Ms. Roberts initiated a conversation with Paul during the same journal-writing period, the focus of attention was quite different. Ms. Roberts engaged Paul in a series of brief conversations clearly directed toward getting him to add to his text, providing both support and raw material for the desired elaboration of his story about Christmas presents. Ms. Roberts got Paul's attention immediately after he had written "boy and girl." She signed BOY. GIRL. #DO #DO? ("What did the boy and girl do?") Paul signed OPEN-A-BOX. Ms. Roberts, "I SEE, OPEN-A-BOX." Paul wrote the English word *open* and then announced, "FINISH!" Ms. Roberts signed, "BOY GIRL OPEN-A-DOOR?" Paul disagreed, shaking his head. Ms. Roberts pursued the topic, WHAT? BOY GIRL OPEN-A-BOX? OPEN-A-DRAWER? Paul disagreed, shook his head, and signed OPEN-A-BOX. T̲RUCK AND DOLL. Ms. Roberts responded, "WONDERFUL! INDEX-paper WRITE." ("Wonderful. Write it there.")

Like Paul, the boys focused on the details of the equivalences between ASL and English and upon the intricacies of the written code. This was not surprising since writing systems in general interested them. In addition, the ability to identify English word equivalents and to write, spell, and locate words in the printed material on bulletin boards was a matter of personal pride for all three of the boys and carried some social prestige as well (e.g., during ad hoc spelling contests). Their focus on forms of equivalence interacted nicely with their ability to invoke a range of language functions during journal writing.

Recall that the mainstreaming classroom afforded deaf students few occasions to interact with others except to the extent that they were on the receiving end of directives and evaluations. In the self-contained classroom, interaction was not only intelligible, it offered Paul, Robbie, and Tom opportunities to accomplish a variety of social and learning activities. Although there was some social contact for the deaf boys in the mainstreaming classroom, it existed on the surface only. The hearing and deaf children devoted minimal energy to interacting with each other, and most of their interactions were negotiations or bids for brief attention. The hearing and deaf children were not friends or playmates, did not really know each other, and did not know what they might have in common. In the self-contained classroom, the three boys were fast friends who knew a great deal about each other's lives outside of school and shared several school years' worth of memories and history.

It is worth pointing out again that this friendship and social life rested in part upon their ability to communicate in a mutually intelligible language. In fact, Robbie and Tom had probably been among Paul's peer socializing agents as he learned to communicate in signing with other children. These three boys, in turn, were socializing a new signer in their class, Lawrence, into the collective of signing peers. Children who do not share a language can make little progress toward social life beyond exploring and negotiating the limited terms upon which they might interact. This seemingly obvious fact has been overlooked in popularized sentimental visions of deaf and hearing children learning together (Ramsey 1994). It is critical to take seriously the intelligibility of interaction through language in the classroom lives of deaf children.

LANGUAGE AS A TOOL

Focusing on language used to accomplish social purposes at school is unusual in conventional deaf education research. Although teachers might establish pragmatic language goals for deaf children, learning the situations in which to apply formulaic utterances is only a narrow slice of learning. At Aspen School, a quiet class like Mrs. Rogers' was the ideal. Vygotskyan theory, however, proposes that social uses for language are not only critical to learning; interaction with others, organized culturally, is where development has its roots. The English title of one of Vygotsky's books is, tellingly, *Mind in Society,* reflecting the claim that the mind is a social and cultural phenomenon rather than solely an individual possession. Accordingly, rather than focus only on the children's opportunities to interact and have friendships with peers, my hypothesis is that Tom, Robbie, and Paul, like all developing children, were transforming the social functions of language into internal intellectual functions that mediated their approach to English and to writing. That is, their experiences taking many roles in conversations and their ability to invoke an array of language functions to accomplish their intentions with others became tools for their thoughts about, as well as their analysis of, written English.

The boys all signed to themselves during the two literacy activities where they were called upon to produce writing—language lessons and journal writing. Their signed comments to themselves were directive (very similar to the directive monitoring, planning, and coding strategies Dyson's (1989) young hearing writers invoked) and personal. That is, the three boys not only planned the details of their drawing and writing by signing to themselves but they also commented on and evaluated their own work as well.

For example, Paul sorted his "feeling word" vocabulary cards into categories by looking at each one and signing to himself, "KNOW-IT" ("I know that."). Tom dawdled through the language lesson period and, as time grew short, signed to himself, "NOT-YET FINISH. THAT-PILE REMAIN" ("I'm not done. I still have those to do."). When Robbie was having a terrible time cutting with the dull school scissors, he set them down and signed to himself, "TOO-HARD. I CAN'T CUT-WITH-SCISSORS. LOUSY CUT-WITH-SCISSORS ME" ("It's too hard. I can't cut this. I'm a lousy cutter."). Observations of children talking audibly to themselves as they tackle challenging tasks are not uncommon (e.g., Dyson 1989), although the signed channel of communication is. Nonetheless, the language the boys used during literacy activities functioned precisely as any human language would, despite its signed form. Just as they could use language to mark membership in various social groups and to gather information about the world, they could use the mediational power of language to tackle new, difficult, or complex tasks.

Tom, Robbie, and Paul conversed with others during journal periods to ask for help, to brag about a drawing, to offer critiques to others, to tell stories, and to gossip. Notably, each boy also signed and fingerspelled to himself as he struggled to write his ideas, often expressed in ASL to classmates and in print English to teachers. Signing to themselves was a tool for accomplishing writing, which had its roots in the interpersonal signing and the social relations that structured their life as signers in the self-contained classroom.

Once a day, right before lunch, the children sat around the outside of the crescent-shaped table for journal time. There were no specific English lessons planned for these periods. The goal, according to Ms. Roberts, was to provide a time when the deaf students could practice getting their ideas out of their heads and onto paper, via whatever means they wished to use. At least one of the adults was always available to help the children, and often all three were present. The children were free to converse with each other, and a variety of resources was available (e.g., word lists, calendars, maps, books, and scratch paper). Any instruction about English or about such matters as the arranging of written text on the page occurred in context, in response to the children's questions or problems with the immediate task.

It is important to describe the knowledge and skills that signing deaf children need in order to write English. As a complex manipulation of symbols, writing for these children is similar to the general task that hearing English-speaking children undertake but with critical complications that hearing children do not face. Thus we are again directed to the contexts in which they learn and practice their skills. Accordingly, in order to approach print, deaf children need access to an intelligible social context that also provides resources for the tasks they are asked to do. An intelligible classroom for profoundly deaf children is one where discourse is structured by a natural sign language used in the ways that native "speakers" organize teaching discourse. There is compelling evidence that ASL is a powerful mediator for deaf children's learning, specifically because it is a natural signed language with a long history of use in Deaf communities (e.g., Padden and Humphries 1988; Lane et al. 1996). ASL is not, however, the only resource signing deaf children need at school. Importantly, another key resource is well-planned instruction in English vocabulary, English grammar, and the structure of written texts. Again the most likely medium of instruction for these topics is ASL. Like any language, ASL can be used to discuss any possible topic. Deaf Americans embed a great deal of knowledge about English in the structure of their language (e.g., Padden in press) as well as in in-group patterns that have evolved over time specifically to engage young signers with English in classroom settings (Ramsey 1996). In addition, there is growing evidence that knowledge of ASL correlates with reading and English ability (Padden and Ramsey in press). Although this relationship has been well known for several decades, a good deal of supporting evidence has accumulated as bilingual/bicultural pedagogies have been developed. In contemporary times the traditional resistance to ASL as a medium of instruction is no longer justified.

Where children have many classroom opportunities to engage with others using a natural language in intelligible, conventional ways, learning and development may unfold. Critical language-use opportunities were notably absent in the mainstreaming classroom. In the self-contained classroom, however, many existed, and both children and adults participated. Each boy had his own way of approaching tasks and utilizing the resources in the classroom, but all three employed strategies for engaging others during writing when they needed assistance or companionship. Importantly, each also acted precisely as theory would predict. Like any child—hearing or deaf—tackling a complex and difficult task like writing, traces of each boy's thinking were external at times—visible in his signing to himself.

Robbie

Robbie explained writing this way: "To write," he signed, "you have to be smart . . . and ask." Indeed, Robbie's actions during writing reflected this. He liked school and knew a lot about how to be smart at school. He embarked on writing tasks without being prodded by an adult and labored to produce English texts. On a rainy spring day, Robbie decided to write a journal entry entitled "The Sun." He began by taking a yellow crayon, looking at his journal page, and signing to himself THINK THINK. Then he drew the sun, with lines depicting orbits around it and circles representing planets. Mrs. Hart, who was supervising journal writing, showed interest in his picture and began an instructional conversation with him. "What planet is that?" she asked. "What's the next one called?" Robbie named EARTH, then fingerspelled M-A-R. He paused and added, C-H. As he spelled C-H, Mrs. Hart caught his eye and spelled R-S, and Robbie grabbed his pencil box to write in the correct word, *Mars*. When Mrs. Hart pointed to the next orb on the picture, Robbie scowled: He could not remember any more planet names. However, he did not ask Mrs. Hart to tell him the names. Instead, from his seat, he scanned the room, looking for a book that might have a picture of the solar system, muttering to himself (in sign) WHERE BOOK? WHERE BOOK? Agreeing that books were very helpful resources, Mrs. Hart went to locate one that he could use. As he finished his drawing, she placed a science book on the table, where Robbie located a map of the solar system.

Among the boys, Robbie was known as a good speller. He frequently offered corrections to friends' texts, reminding Paul, for example, that writing *two sister* was wrong: If there were two, then Paul had to add an *s* to *sister* to make it right. Although Robbie volunteered information and provided unsolicited instruction about writing to his peers, when he required assistance himself he never asked peers for help but always turned to an adult; interestingly, he often used his voice in his attempts to solicit information about English. Robbie's selective use of his voice is intriguing, especially since he denied speaking, claimed that he never used his voice, and pouted and moped when the speech teacher came to pull him out for speech lessons. His use of his voice in soliciting help from signing people during literacy activities suggested that he had included spoken pronunciation of words as one feature of literacy tasks that he could exploit under very specific circumstances. That is, this strategy was useful only when his interlocutor could both talk and sign and was otherwise known to him as a helpful, supportive adult. He refused to employ this sound resource when the interlocutor did not sign. When requesting information from adults during writing time, Robbie used speech to specify the exact word he wanted to know. For example, as he wrote his solar system text, he turned to Mrs. Hart and signed REAL. SPELL REAL. The first REAL was only signed. On the second he made an attempt to pronounce the word *real*. Mrs. Hart, using sign and speech, replied REAL O-R REAL ("true or real"), asking him to specify the English word. He insisted with sign and voice that he meant *real*.

In addition to the heuristic language Robbie invoked during writing, he conversed with others to recount stories and to share factual information. He engaged with Tom and Robbie for several purposes. For example, he leaned over to look at Tom's drawing of Uncle Scrooge and signed approvingly, MY FAVORITE. Later, Robbie and Paul gossiped in ASL about Tom's dreamy behavior and speculated about "third-grade paper" with narrower lines and no space for drawing. Since Robbie's preference was to be "smart" and solve his spelling and writing problems on his own, he frequently signed to himself directively to monitor and plan his writing. Clearly visible, his thinking and planning during writing activities included such strategic actions as counting on his fingers to calculate the date and dictating to himself using signs and very soft sounds as he wrote words. Placed in the context of his in-progress writing, his dictation also suggested his current notion about writing English. For example, he wrote a cautionary message in his journal. He began with "don't," then added "go to sun will die you." Upon silently rereading this line, he erased "don't" and replaced it with "do you don't." His text now read: "The sun is real solar system. Do you don't go to sun will die you." He reconsidered his sentence once again, signing each word carefully, uttering soft noises on "do" and "go." Then he erased "you" and moved it so that the sentence finally read: "Do you don't go to sun will you die." As soon as he completed this revision, Robbie began making bids for Mrs. Hart's attention to announce that he was finished writing.

These small adjustments to his written text were not random, and they did not involve searches for specific lexical items to add meaning to his journal entry. Robbie's carefully considered revisions, which he signed and "talked" himself through, reflected attempts to make his writing conform better to a written representation of English. Although the end product is far from conventional, young deaf writers' products do not transparently reflect the intentional processes that created them. Robbie also signed to himself to assist his recall. As he worked on his text, Robbie announced to Mrs. Hart in ASL, I KNOW. SUN VERY HOT. He then wrote "sun is v," then stopped and signed to himself HARD. VERY HARD. This utterance could have been a comment on the task he was facing (although it did not appear that he was finding it difficult). More likely, however, he was recalling another familiar phrase where the word *very* appeared. Immediately after this utterance, he looked at the word list on the bulletin board, located *very* and finished his sentence.

When Mrs. Hart accepted Robbie's written journal entry and certified that it was truly finished (primarily because it consisted of at least twenty words), he resumed work on his diagram of the solar system. Looking at the map of the solar system in the book he was using, he signed to himself, INDEX-planet on his map NEXT ("That one's next."). Paul looked over at

Robbie's drawing and signed to himself, I REMEMBER INDEX-planet on map ("I remember that one."). To Robbie, he commented INDEX-planet DEAD. BREATHE THAT-ONE NEED MASK ("That one is dead. To breathe on that one you need a mask."). Robbie responded with excitement INDEX-planet COLD WOW REALLY. INDEX-another planet YOU CAN'T SEE ("That one is really really cold. You can't see that one."). He traced the orbit of the planet, shaking his head. Paul nodded his head in agreement.

After this moment of friendship and science, Robbie looked with pride at his drawing. Abruptly he signed to himself HEY! I FORGET MOON. FORGET MOON. FORGET MOON. BLANK-THERE INDEX-drawing ("Hey. I forgot the moon! There's nothing there on the drawing."). Mrs. Hart, who had seen his signing, got his attention and suggested he add the moon. Robbie nodded his head and signed seriously to her, REAL MOON ("This is the moon."). Drawing the moon near the earth, he carefully added orbit lines around the sun for each of the planets in his drawing. Several minutes passed, and again Robbie stopped drawing to admire his work. Paul reached over and signed, REMEMBER? DIRT? DIRT AND ROCK. MANY MANY ROCK INDEX-outer space ("Remember? There's all that dirt and rocks flying through outer space."). Robbie responded, I KNOW-IT. THERE. He added rocks to his depiction of outer space. As he drew, Tom and Paul cleared away their materials and went to lunch. Robbie continued to embellish his solar system a few minutes longer and was the last to leave the table. His journal entry read:

> The sun is Real Solar
> system Do you Don't
> go to sun will you
> Die sun is very Hot.

Tom

In second grade, Tom disliked school and viewed writing and reading as difficult tasks not only for deaf children but for hearing children as well. Tom and Robbie both held the belief that the hearing children could not read well because they could not fingerspell—an ability that the deaf boys assumed had something to do with reading. Robbie denied that speech had any relation to reading. (The boys' speculations on hearing students' language and literacy habits are described in detail in Ramsey [in press].) Where Robbie treated print as a puzzle to be solved, Tom regarded it as dangerous territory. When asked about writing at school, he reported with gravity, "Mrs. Hart makes me write because she's mean. And I make mistakes." Tom's dislike of school and the bothersome tasks that Mrs. Hart set for him did not mean that he spent his school days in a symbolic wasteland. Although he was known to the other deaf children as a good storyteller as well as a dreamer (a very unflattering characterization among these school-wise children), he regarded himself as a creative person who adored making things up. During journal time, he preferred to draw and routinely attempted to violate conventions like the "write first, draw second" rule. He often locked horns with Mrs. Hart about other journal time rules, including the always contentious choice of topics. They engaged in daily (mostly good-natured) tussles where Tom's attempts to win his struggles with the adults, especially Mrs. Hart, provided practice in reasoning, disputing, and logic. A creatively resistant student, he had, by only second grade, formed the opinion that writing was the quicksand of school activities, and he skirted it whenever possible.

One day in April the adults selected the topic for journal writing. The task they gave the children was to review their new knowledge about Central America and then to write on a topic that had "something to do with Guatemala." Tom received the special caution that the topic was not to be "pretend." "I know everyday we make up what we write," Ms. Roberts consoled him after his first run-in with Mrs. Hart, "but today what she says is right. Sometimes we make it up, sometimes it's real. Both are important. Today there's no choice. Mrs. Hart is right. Today it's important to write about Guatemala." To his dismay, Tom had to report facts that he had learned about Guatemala during their social studies unit without the support of superheroes or Disney characters.

During this writing period, Tom gathered additional evidence to support his contention that Mrs. Hart was "mean." He did not accept the task of writing something "not pretend" about Guatemala gracefully. Instead, he spent five minutes signing to Mrs. Roberts, explaining his ideas about combining Guatemalan fireworks with superhero attire, for an exciting effect. Carefully outlining his idea, he would design his superheroes' armor (HARD CLOTHING) with built-in fireworks so that fighters' arms would send off flames and sparks. Ms. Roberts agreed that it was a very dramatic idea, then she reminded him that his writing today must be "not pretend," asked him to begin writing, and turned him over to Mrs. Hart. She reopened negotiations on a suitable writing topic. Tom's first idea was to write about the way pop is sold in Guatemala. He signed, POP. OPEN-A-BOTTLE, POUR-INTO-A-BAGGY, STICK-IN-A-STRAW. Mrs. Hart did not consider this a good topic because the existence of pop was not a feature unique to Guatemala. She responded WE HAVE POP. PEOPLE THERE G-U-A-T-E-M-A-L-A HAVE POP. WHAT DIFFERENT? WHAT? ("We have pop. People in Guatemala have pop. What is different about Guatemala?")

Tom protested that he would make up his own topic about POP AND F-I-R-E-W-O-R-K-S AND MASKS, claiming that his topic was NOT PRETEND. He turned away and muttered to himself in ASL, I WANT CREATE. I KISS-HAND. I KISS-HAND CREATE. I KISS-HAND ("I want to make things up. I love it. I love making things up. I love it."). He repeated his complaint to Mrs. Hart, reasoning that his chosen topic *was* about Guatemala. Finally, Mrs. Hart approved Tom's topic: pop in a baggy. (Tom was very interested in what he had seen during the slide show—people drinking pop out of little plastic bags. He had learned that in Guatemala merchants pour a newly purchased bottle of pop into a plastic bag so that customers do not pay a deposit and the merchant keeps the bottles.)

Although his negotiation of a writing topic consisted of well-employed representational language, once Tom began writing, he used language as a tool to get information about equivalents between signing and words. Unlike Robbie, who liked to work alone and asked only for the spellings of specific words, Tom took full advantage of the fact that his primary interlocutors knew both ASL and English, that is, they understood his communication and were repositories of pertinent information. He began his first sentence by copying the long, difficult foreign word *Guatemala* off the board. He wrote "Guatemala have." He stopped, reread his words, and plotted his next move. (In the following examples, Tom substituted the sign for *Spain* rather than fingerspell *Guatemala*). SPAIN, he nodded his head. SPAIN HAVE, he read and signed to himself, HAVE POP. He nodded his head, POP. Then he looked at Mrs. Hart and signed POP. Mrs. Hart pointed to the word *Coke* that was already written on the board. Tom looked at the board and began fingerspelling to himself P-O-P P-O-P. The letters *C-o-k-e* on the board did not match what he knew was the English word *pop*. So what did they mean? He looked at Mrs. Hart, who explained the hierarchical relation between the words *pop* and *Coke*, that there are many kinds of pop and that Coke, with which Tom was very familiar, is one of them. Tom added "Coke" to his sentence, which now read "Guatemala have coke."

In this case, both English words mapped onto the same ASL lexical item. The problem was to determine how the English words related to each other, a task Tom and Mrs. Hart solved between them. However, his next writing task entailed a more complex equivalence relation. As noted earlier, the three boys were beginning to be aware that a complex ASL sign sometimes required several English words or even a sentence to translate. As Tom asked Mrs. Hart for help, he signed (translated here), "You know, you know, a baggy with a straw poked in it? A bag you hold and poke with a straw and drink through the straw? You know? You poke the straw in and drink? How do you spell that?"

Tom's query led to a situation that recurred in the self-contained classroom. At times, Mrs. Hart's confidence in her command of English failed her. Like the children (and like many of us who use a second language with some fluency but cannot easily translate from our mother tongue into our second language), she had difficulty translating between ASL and English. Sometimes she declined to help the children spell English words or translate from signing into print and deferred to the hearing teachers, who were both native speakers of English. From her example, the boys routinely got glimpses of the reality of Deaf people's relation to their written language, English. They not only saw Deaf and hearing people cooperating and successfully communicating, they also could observe that it was permissible to ask for help with spelling. They noticed the reciprocal reality of hearing and Deaf people interacting around ASL as well. There were multiple opportunities to observe the hearing signers asking Mrs. Hart questions about ASL and about the lives of Deaf people. Conversations built around specific questions about English and ASL demonstrated that communication and the specifics of languages were potential and permissible topics of conversations. They served as well to repeatedly name the two languages and elaborate on the distinctions between their forms and functions in Deaf people's lives.

In response to Tom's request for the "spelling" of "a bag you hold and poke with a straw and drink through the straw," Ms. Roberts fingerspelled a gloss for him, "bag with straw." With some difficulty, Tom added this phrase to his text, griping repeatedly that Ms. Roberts and Mrs. Hart fingerspelled too fast. (Although Ms. Roberts might have provided Tom with the standard written string "a bag with a straw poked in it," she chose to give him "bag with straw." Her reason for doing so was most likely to satisfy his request as rapidly as possible in the interest of furthering his progress on his journal entry, rather than interrupting his momentum with a lengthy explanation more suited to "language lesson" period).

Although Tom asked for and received the help he needed during journal writing, most of his signing was not directed to others. The bulk of his signing was to himself—and much of it was personal—to express his feelings and attitudes (Dyson 1989, p. 286) about the social situation and the task. Tom often used personal signing to express his displeasure with Mrs. Hart and Ms. Roberts. He uttered small signs, close to his chest, that did not appear to be directed to any interlocutor, and when doing so, he did not make eye contact with any of his classmates.

As noted above, after Mrs. Hart told him that he must write about Guatemala, he muttered to himself, grousing about his desire to make things up. Later, after another difficult negotiation with Mrs. Hart about the many new facts he supposedly had learned about Guatemala, he signed to himself, I CAN'T REMEMBER. I NOT SEE-IT. A second personal function that Tom invoked was playing with the shapes and movements of signs, just as hearing children might discover and play with appealing combinations of spoken sounds. Tom created whimsical refrains, repeating signs to himself while he took breaks from writing. For example, he languidly signed to himself STRAW STRAW after he wrote "straw." Later, after he failed to get Ms. Roberts's attention for a needed spelling, he repeatedly signed to himself SPELL KISS-HAND as he waited for her to look at him.

Tom's signing to himself was also directive, invoking monitoring, planning, and reviewing functions during the difficult task of composing and putting a text into print. With one exception, all of his directive signing took place while he wrote about Coke in Guatemala. The exception was an intentional attempt to generate a sentence during his prolonged negotiation over a journal topic. After he suggested writing about F-I-R-E-W-O-R-K-S, Mrs. Hart challenged him to come up with a sentence (that is, evidence that he actually had something to write about fireworks), then looked away to converse with another student. Tom thought for a moment and laboriously and deliberately signed to himself, FIRE SCARE ME. BULL . . . He shook his head and began again. BULL IS . . . (using a sign from one of the manual codes for English). He did not attempt to write either of these sentences. Instead, he paused briefly, turned to Mrs. Hart, and once again tried to make a case for his preferred topic, "I know! I know, I know! They have pop in a bag, they drink out of the bag with a straw!" Tom's attempt to sign a sentence is notable for two reasons. First, he did not attempt to commit these strings to print. His "sentences" were a performance in response to a directive from Mrs. Hart, and his insertion of *is* was an indication of his current notion of what a sentence signed as a performance might require. This somewhat empty use of an "English" sign did not lead anywhere in his literacy activity. In fact, during writing Tom did not take many risks with English. Unlike Robbie, he did not experiment with the order of words in a string. When he wanted to write, his main concern was translating into print the ideas that he signed. His texts, sequences of clear, simple sentences, reflected this.

Second, this was the only time during this journal activity that Tom intentionally used a lexical item from a manual code for English (MCE). This example illustrates a feature of the functional distribution of languages exhibited by all three boys. For face-to-face interaction, they used their developing ASL almost exclusively. The only times any lexical items from manual codes for English appeared in their signing was during literacy activities, when a very small set of MCE lexical items leaked into discourse. The most common were *the, is, -ing,* and *-s*. It is important to note, however, that these signs were used sparingly and did not appear to support or to serve in any mediating fashion the move between the language used face-to-face and English print. The children used ASL pronominal reference and avoided the pronoun signs from the contrived English systems (e.g., *I, he, she, it, we, they*).

As he wrote, Tom followed a complex functional pattern of signing directively to himself, which included visible dictation to himself in advance of writing as well as plotting his next idea by rereading what he had just written. He constantly moved between print and fingerspelling, translating ASL signs to English print words, and deciding between competing terms. Tom looked over what he had written: "Guatemala have coke and have bag with straw and Tom have. . . ." He shook his head and, while erasing *have* with his right hand, signed LIKE, KISS-HAND, LIKE, KISS-HAND with his left hand. He was trying to decide which term to use. LIKE is a less strong term of affection than KISS-HAND, which roughly translates to "love" or "adore." He decided on the stronger term KISS-HAND and wrote "love coke." He then screamed "Yeah!!" and wrote "and my friend love coke." Feeling triumphant (and desperate to be finished with writing), he signed FINISHED!! with satisfaction. Failing to get Mrs. Hart's attention, he reread his text and began laughing as he neared the final words. Giggling he signed to himself, FRIEND. FRIEND LOVE. Mrs. Hart looked over, and he announced again, FINISHED!!

Mrs. Hart reminded him of the journal writing rule: "finished" meant your text had to be twenty words long. And, she added ominously, RECESS ("It's nearly recess time"). Tom counted each word of his text, uttering each number sign by placing his hand on his paper, "One, two, three, . . . seventeen!" "Think of another sentence," signed Mrs. Hart. Tom began composing to himself I KISS-HAND. I KISS-HAND. I DON'T KNOW. He gazed around the table, stared at his paper for ten seconds, then slowly and deliberately signed BUT . . . BUT POP. Then his face lit up and he wrote "but Tom." Getting Mrs. Hart to help him write "know," he reread his text and added "coke have." Then he signed to himself TOM KNOW POP HAVE SUGAR, and to Mrs. Hart he signed SPELL SUGAR. With her help, he wrote the last word, *sugar,* happily signed FINISHED! and went to recess. Tom's journal entry about Guatemala read:

> Guatemala have coke and have bag with straw
> and I love coke and my friend love coke
> but Tom know coke have sugar.

Paul

Of the three boys, Paul was the most recent to acquire language and to use print. He turned nine early in the study year and had begun to learn to sign only three years before. The teachers reported that during first grade (the year before the study) he did not sign much. According to Ms. Roberts, "something clicked" during second grade, and the adults were very pleased with the increase in his willingness to communicate and his growing interest in language. Paul himself seemed to be aware of his growth. He reported, "I love to write. It's my favorite." Wildly proud when he memorized a spelling list, for example, he often tried to engage adults in spelling games.

However, his grip on writing confidence was tenuous, and almost by reflex, at the beginning of journal writing one day in February, he signed to Lawrence SCHOOL. SPELL SCHOOL. As Lawrence responded, S S-C-H, Paul began giggling, shook his head, and lifted up a book to cover his face. Then he confidently wrote "school" in his journal. Despite his growing confidence, Paul was accustomed to not knowing how to spell all of the words he wanted to write. However, he appeared to remember part way through Lawrence's help that he could spell and write the word by himself, so he blocked out Lawrence's fingerspelling by covering his own face with a book and continued without further assistance.

Although not yet a skilled signer, Paul maneuvered well through the social life of writing time. He asked for and accepted assistance from both peers and adults. One obstacle he faced was getting the attention of potential interlocutors, a common experience that confronted those new to signed discourse (Ramsey and Padden 1996). He often tried to initiate a conversation, got no response, then sat quietly and waited for someone to respond to him, as other people around him continued signed conversations. When he was engaged in writing, Paul worked with great concentration and disliked being bothered or interrupted. He had learned to use stern, explicit language with his peers during literacy activities. For example, when Tom disengaged from school work and sought a playmate or someone to tell stories to or giggle with, Paul routinely looked him in the eye and signed, STOP. I IGNORE YOU ("Stop it. I'm going to ignore you."). When Tom was being especially irritating, Paul and Robbie openly gossiped about him and shared their disapproval of his dreamy, silly ways.

Like Robbie, Paul treated print as a puzzle-solving activity. Other than his stern responses to Tom's silliness, he approached the social setting of writing with pleasure, especially when Mrs. Hart was at the table. He engaged easily with her animated style of signing. For example, during Paul's February journal writing event, he chose two topics from a box of story starters provided by the teachers to keep the boys from writing constantly about superheroes. He could not read either of them: "Fun with a sled" and "I can't believe my eyes." He didn't know the word *sled* (he had never lived in a snowy climate) and was unfamiliar with the expression "can't believe my eyes." He began reading the latter aloud with signs, expressing each word with the correct sign. However, he stopped and self-corrected several times before finishing the whole phrase, perhaps because the string of signs did not make sense to him.

Taking this opportunity to translate the English expression through drama, Mrs. Hart held up the slip of paper and signed, as the boys giggled, MEAN WHAT? INDEX-imaginary object in the room LOOK-OVER-THERE! W-O-W!! LOOK-OVER-THERE! ("What does this mean? Look! Over there! Wow!! Look over there!") INDEX-story starter paper MEAN WHAT? I CAN'T BELIEVE IT ("What does this paper mean? It means 'I can't believe it.'"). Paul engaged with her imaginary surprise and signed, "Wow! It's (the imaginary object) so pretty!" Despite this amusing English lesson and his very limited knowledge of snow, Paul decided to write on the topic of "fun with a sled."

Paul began by writing "School"; then he added the phrase, "when finish go to home play Nintendo," diligently using previous journal entries as a model for his sentences as well as a glossary for spelling the words. As Paul wrote, he signed with Lawrence and Mrs. Hart to get help with his writing. Like Robbie, Paul asked for help by asking about individual words. However, Paul was a less experienced signer than Robbie and sometimes made pronunciation errors that derailed his search for written equivalents for signs. He signed to himself, rereading and planning, WHEN FINISH GO . . . GO TO SEATTLE. Then he asked Mrs. Hart to spell SEATTLE. Then he wrote a solitary S. His text now read, "School when finish to go S." He picked up the tiny slip of paper where his topic was printed, pointed to the s in *sled*, and signed again to Mrs. Hart a sign that appeared to be the sign name for SEATTLE. Mrs. Hart, trying but failing to connect Paul's request to his "fun with a sled" topic, asked for clarification, SEATTLE? GO TO SEATTLE? WHY? BECAUSE CITY? OK. She wrote *Seattle* on a piece of scratch paper and gave it to Paul. He completed the word *Seattle* in his journal, looked over his writing, slapped his forehead, started giggling and erased *eattle*. Then he took the piece of scratch paper, scrunched it up, and put it in his mouth. Mrs. Hart watched in confusion as Paul looked at her and shook his head. Her response was, SEATTLE. YOU SAY SEATTLE. YOU SIGN S. I NOT UNDERSTAND. Mrs. Hart explained that she was confused, that Paul had signed SEATTLE (an S handshape, palm facing forward, uttered with a small left to right shaking movement). Paul made use of the print resources in the room (as Robbie did) and scanned the walls, pointing finally to the area where a map of the United States and a calendar were tacked to the wall. OK, she signed, GO-TO MAP. Paul took his journal and a pencil and went to look closely not at the map but at the calendar. He carefully copied *satur* into his journal and returned to the table. After he was settled, he added *day* from memory to his text. He sat back, looked at his text, and tapped "day" with his pencil. Mrs. Hart signed OH YOU WANT SATURDAY. Then she demonstrated the difference between SEATTLE and SATURDAY (SEATTLE has palm orientation away from the body, whereas SATURDAY has palm orientation facing the body).

The entire interaction, beginning with Paul's appearing to sign to himself GO TO SEATTLE (although what he wanted to write was "go to Saturday"), through Mrs. Hart's help, the discovery of the misunderstanding, and Paul's and Mrs. Hart's actions to correct it, demonstrated yet again ways that the self-contained classroom provided multiple tools for gaining access to others, procuring information about language, resolving confusion, and gaining control of writing, even for a beginning signer like Paul.

Several theoretically intriguing phenomena took place during Paul's trouble with SEATTLE and SATURDAY, two conventional signs whose similar forms confused Paul. Despite this, Paul signaled with intention to Mrs. Hart that he was looking for a written word that began with *s*. When the interaction became confused and Paul could not resolve the misunderstanding with language, he used pointing and movement about the room to communicate and get what he wanted. Mrs. Hart supplied the linguistic communication in ASL; in essence, she shouldered most of the communicational burden and was the one who put both Paul's wishes and his confusion into language. Mrs. Hart also made the form of ASL signs—specifically the feature of palm orientation—explicit in order to help Paul understand how the misunderstanding took place. Perhaps because he had been without rich language interaction for his first five years, he was good at making use of resources to get what he needed. At the same time, he was fortunate to be in a classroom where others put forth effort toward clearing up confusion as well as explaining its cause.

The writing that Paul produced in this segment, "go to Saturday," suggests that in addition to experimenting with the forms of signs and the possible representational relations they could have with print, he was also operating with rules about what written English must include. Paul confidently planned and wrote "go," then reflected upon his text so far and added "to." The fact that he wanted to write about what he did on Saturday, rather than going to a place, did not affect his intentional use of "go to." It is possible that this phrase marked "English" or "writing" to him, especially since it appeared in his previous entry ("go to home").

Near the end of his journal writing, Mrs. Hart again used exaggeration and joking to make a point about English. Paul had written "School when finish go to Saturday snow fun. Sled brother." He leaned back in his chair with a sigh, admiring his text. Mrs. Hart read his text: SLED BROTHER? YOU MEAN WITH BROTHER? ("sled brother? You mean *with* brother?") She explained in ASL that his sentence suggested that his brother is a sled and that he rode on his brother's back. She dramatically signed what that would mean, that Paul had been sliding down the hill using his brother as a sled. Twice she reasoned her way through this with Paul, then explained using ASL, "you say *with* brother," and showed him where to insert *with*. By this time, Paul was laughing loudly. He stopped long enough to find the paper with his original journal topic, "Fun with a sled." He looked at it carefully, pointed to *with*, and copied it into his journal in the place Mrs. Hart indicated. (Again, it is unclear why Mrs. Hart did not help Paul to write the more standard string "with my brother.") Mrs. Hart once more looked over Paul's written text, announced it complete, and told him he could draw a picture. He grabbed a crayon and began to draw an illustration for his text about sledding. From time to time he turned back to previous journal entries, spruced up other illustrations, and laughed as he reviewed previous entries. Having finished his drawing, he closed his journal and gave it to Mrs. Hart, who asked him to read his journal entry to her. He opened to his "sled" entry and signed each word to her. She nodded and commented that now it said that he was sitting on a sled, not on his brother. This is Paul's text:

> School when finish
> go to SaTURday
> snow fun Sled with
> brother

As journal time came to a close, Mrs. Hart noticed that all of the pages of Paul's journal book were filled. She asked, "Do you want to take it home? You have to read it all to me first." Very pleased to have completed his journal book, he happily read every entry to Mrs. Hart, who praised his hard work and good drawing. Paul left the table to pack the journal book into his book bag.

Robbie, Tom, and Paul were active social beings who observed the world around them at school and engaged in strategic activities during writing. As they worked, they discovered and created relationships between their social lives in the self-contained classroom, their internal mental lives, and their written products. Among these children, face-to-face language and written language interacted in complex and important ways. The social resources of the deaf classroom, built around signing, contributed to their attempts to discover and create a relationship with their face-to-face signing and written English. Through the use of ASL, the adults engaged the boys in school activities and ensured participation. The boys, in turn, were developing two critical abilities. They could reflect upon language and communication as objects of attention. Importantly, they could also invoke the mediating power of language as a tool for learning.

Chapter 7

Placements, Contexts, and Consequences

The Aspen School deaf and hard of hearing program manifests the true nature of public school programs for deaf children. The contrast between the mainstreaming placement and the self-contained class context teaches an important lesson. We cannot deeply understand the measured academic problems of deaf students without discerning the societal roots of the institutions where they are schooled and the local social forces that structure their school days. The stories of Tom, Robbie, and Paul—which move from their school and mainstreaming class to their self-contained class and finally to their processes of using language as a tool—are comprehensible only when they are located in time and place. They are the clients of American-style deaf education in the late twentieth century, at a time when the field has undergone several rapid changes in ideology, from oralism to total communication to bilingual/bicultural pedagogy and from separate schools to local, integrated school placements. The boys are not unfortunate individuals who cannot hear and who struggle in school. They are, rather, members of a group: deaf children with hearing families who love them and want the best for them, who must make decisions on their behalf in a climate of change without knowing what the outcomes will be. In all likelihood, Tom, Robbie, and Paul will also become Deaf as they approach young adulthood. They represent the majority of deaf students in the United States, and it is this group that deserves attention because it shoulders the consequences of deaf education ideology and innovations.

Special education alternatives are often termed "options," as if it were possible to make a rational and objective selection from a set of equally good choices. This was the idea that bolstered mainstreaming among administrators at Aspen School. After making a rational offering of a schooling program, they formulated placement decisions. At this point, they believed their work was done and their obligation to the deaf students and their parents complete. As Ms. Roberts's supervisor reminded her, she did not have to provide the best education for her students. She simply had to provide an adequate education so that the students could "make it." Nevertheless, actually having deaf students in mainstreaming classes at Aspen School was not a simple matter, and the jury is still out on whether we can characterize the boys' mainstreaming experiences as evidence that they were succeeding. Not only was there no training and little preparation for receiving teachers, there was little notion that they needed to do anything beyond work with an interpreter to include the deaf children at Aspen School's regular classes. District-level statements and everyday actions at the school made it clear that the mainstreaming placements were only marginally educational for the deaf students. Rather, a not uncommon and completely well-meaning noneducational attitude governed many teachers' views of the deaf children in the mainstream. Not only did they believe that was it good for the hearing children to be with the disabled children, they also believed that this generation of children would grow up to be kinder and more understanding toward disabled people and that the future world would be a more integrated and humane place. All of these hopes were balanced on the shoulders of a group of very young children with critical developmental and educational needs that could barely be addressed in mainstreaming settings.

The self-contained classroom was organized according to a contrasting ideology, in some ways as abstract, optimistic, and remote from teaching as the mainstreaming ideology. Teachers of the deaf face a complication of practice that will never disappear. Most deaf children have hearing parents who do not sign and who have never met a deaf person. The reconciliation of hearing, English-speaking individuals and deaf ASL-signing persons is difficult to accomplish even among adults. In families with young children, this reconciliation is even more complicated and problematic. With a child's intellectual development, indeed, perhaps with her or his entire school career on the line, what can it mean to parents to learn that their deaf child is destined to be a member of an unfamiliar cultural and language group? How can a culturally friendly pedagogy of deaf education ever be put in place in a demographic context that re-creates the community of Deaf people with virtually every generation?

This is the set of beliefs that organized the self-contained classroom and characterized the dilemma that Ms. Roberts, Ms. Adams, and Mrs. Hart confronted daily. Although they had assimilated the cultural account of deaf education, like most others who have moved in this direction, they did not completely understand how to put it into practice. Indeed, classroom practices do not immediately emerge from a cultural ideology about deafness, despite its great intuitive appeal. They understood that children must use language to learn it, which put them ahead of many of their professional colleagues. Yet the more immediate linguistic emergency of early childhood deafness—providing the children with signed language exposure and practice—was the focus of their attention; at the same time, their training and experience structured their actions. Accordingly, the children were offered an unusually rich environment for learning ASL in the public school. In addition, they learned important strategies for moving between ASL and English.

With a native signer, Mrs. Hart, as their guide, they were learning to reflect on language as well as to use languages as tools. Yet, teaching English was not afforded as much attention, a circumstance that is not uncommon. Ms. Roberts and her coteachers faced many constraints that contributed to their limited English teaching. First, their school day with the deaf students was short. They had $3\frac{1}{2}$–4 hours a day to conduct their classroom life, maintain a sense of community, have book sharing, journal writing, and language lessons, and then squeeze in topics required by both the children's individualized educational plans (IEPs) and by the school. The deaf children had pull-out sessions with the speech teacher and with the school counselor, never scheduled during mainstreaming and always cutting into the self-contained class time. In addition, Ms. Roberts and Ms. Adams were obligated to participate in schoolwide initiatives and hence had to include self-esteem lessons as well as anti-AIDS and antidrug presentations. A second constraint was the pressure to use school district second-grade materials and to finish them during second grade so that the deaf children would be able to move smoothly into third grade and third-grade materials. The teachers of the deaf saw through this curricular illusion and knew that their students could neither read nor understand the second-grade materials as the native English-speaking students could. Accordingly, they spent much time working on activities that were designed to fill in the most immediate gaps in the children's science and social studies knowledge not only so they could engage with the materials but also so they could begin to find their places in the world around them.

The introduction poses questions that form the foundation for progressive deaf education: Why are intelligible language, social interaction, and access to the deaf cultural group important? What benefits can we gain from regarding classrooms as contexts rather than as places? Teachers, especially ones like Ms. Roberts and Ms. Adams, who have moved toward a bilingual/bicultural pedagogy need to regard their teaching practice as offering access to intelligible language and Deaf people's history as a group. In addition, however, they also need to understand and to help others understand that classrooms are not simply neutral and interchangeable locations within a school building. Rather than fretting about the restrictiveness of one class over another, a feature that can hardly be measured, parents, administrators, and school personnel must begin to see classrooms as contexts designed for a purpose: children's development and learning. Contexts for deaf children's development and learning must be designed with their needs in mind. One of the native signers commented that the self-contained classroom (which he watched on videotape) was "better than most mainstreaming programs." And he was right. Although life and instruction in the self-contained classroom was never perfect, Ms. Roberts and Ms. Adams carefully and deliberately planned activities and assembled personnel that would contribute to the context they wanted to create, a combination of activities, languages, behavior, and people that was designed especially for deaf children. The mainstreaming classroom, like many such placements, was not a context designed to promote deaf children's learning. When teachers come to understand the importance of intelligible and engaging schooling for deaf children and the richness of the cultural patterns of literacy, language use, and knowledge transmission of the Deaf community, mainstreaming placements like Mrs. Rogers' classroom will be seen for what they are: physical, but not intellectual or spiritual, proximity of deaf and hearing children that serves limited educational purposes.

From a theoretical perspective, the boys' activities in the self-contained classroom provide an intriguing view of deaf children's curiosity about language, their determination to solve the puzzles of print, and their potential to engage with high-quality English and literacy instruction. It was very clear that they could regard their languages as objects. They not only made languages a topic of discussion, they also took a metalinguistic stance toward writing, regarding their written productions of English as objects that could be manipulated, commented upon, and repaired with intention. Notably, they were learning to use language as a tool, and their signing to themselves during the difficult task of writing suggests that they were not only struggling with the task, but they were also working through it using the mental and social resources at hand. From my observations, the boys were certainly capable of engaging with English instruction. They were curious about language, and importantly, Robbie and Paul were meticulous writers who wanted their written words and texts to be correct. Such children are perfect candidates for well-designed language arts instruction that exploits their knowledge of ASL, their desire to produce good work, and their pride in their accomplishments.

My stance toward routine integration of deaf students should be clear. The mere placement of deaf and hearing children in the same room is a waste of deaf children's developmental time and a thoughtless burden to place on them. At Aspen School no educational goals were achieved in the mainstream that could not have been achieved in the self-contained classroom more efficiently and more comprehensibly. The political and social goals of mainstreaming also were unfulfilled. In their interactions with the deaf students, the hearing children at Aspen School reflected what they had learned about their peers with disabilities. The deaf children were akin to mascots in regular classrooms, and the hearing children acted as stern but benevolent caretakers. Unless a school principal and teaching staff can make a commitment to preparing themselves to communicate with and understand the educational needs of deaf children, simply scheduling periods of integration is a fruitless exercise in logistics. Unless they receive education that is designed for them and comprehensible, profoundly deaf children whose dominant language is signed rather than spoken will have a very difficult time acquiring the basic skills they need for a school career in the brief time available to them in the early grades. If students cannot engage with instruction and with others, it is hard to imagine how they will be able to acquire language and school skills.

There is a joke that is periodically revived about a woman who has three plants. She sings to the plants, and two of them grow tall and sprout glossy leaves. Worried about the third plant, she takes it to a "plant doctor." After a careful examination, the plant doctor announces that the plant has failed to thrive because it is deaf and cannot hear her singing. My father, a hearing person, told me this version of the story. Within weeks, a deaf person told me the same joke with an important twist. In the deaf version of the joke, the plant doctor makes another diagnosis. After announcing that the plant is deaf, he explains that it has failed to thrive because it has been mainstreamed.

What do Deaf people know about being mainstreamed that hearing people do not know? They understand the illusion of mainstreaming and know that physical integration, even with an interpreter, does not mean that they can fully participate. In elementary school, mainstreamed deaf children not only find it difficult to participate. In actuality, the barriers to their participation create conditions that *reduce* their opportunities to communicate and interact with hearing students, precisely what mainstreaming is supposed to ensure.

Robbie's, Tom's, and Paul's second-grade careers at Aspen School reflect the difficulties of educating deaf children in public schools. The contrasts between their mainstreaming and self-contained classes presented here, however, provide only a hint of a very complicated situation for both students and teachers. To clarify, the deaf and hard of hearing program at Aspen School was neither a terrible nor a perfect program for deaf students. All in all it was typical, fraught with the problems that many public school programs face. That is, Ms. Roberts and Ms. Adams had an extremely diverse group of deaf and hard of hearing primary students, for whom they had to schedule mainstreaming time as well as basic skills instruction, preteaching, and reviews in the self-contained class. Their students were a typical mix of deaf and hard of hearing children with different interests, attention spans, and communication preferences.

The administration of the Aspen School program was typical also. Although the program had existed for five years, very limited efforts were devoted to preparing teachers and students to have deaf children in their midst. In addition, the program was not regarded as a permanent part of the school, and there was no long-term commitment to maintaining it there. Just as deaf children are often viewed as children with no history and limited connections to the world, their school program was not recognized as having a bona fide connection to the school or a history. Nor did it have a future, as it turned out. The year of the study of Ms. Roberts's and Ms. Adams's classroom was the last year Aspen School was the site of the deaf and hard of hearing program. At the district level, administrators decided to close the program, return all neighboring students to their home districts, and redistribute the district students as well as the staff to other schools. Ms. Roberts, who had already planned to retire, ended her teaching career that year. Ms. Adams, a highly trained and skilled teacher of the deaf, was placed in a resource room in another elementary school, working with students with disabilities. There were no deaf students at that school. Within a year, she left the district and the area and took a job teaching in a day school for deaf students in a large metropolitan district. Mrs. Hart, disheartened at the thought of no longer working with deaf children, also retired.

The children moved through their elementary years in local school district programs. Paul's military family moved to their next post. Tom, always a resistant student, continued to have trouble in school. Robbie's parents made the difficult decision to place him in a public school where he was fully mainstreamed with an interpreter. This school offered a resource teacher but did not have a program for deaf students. Robbie's mother reports that when he entered middle school, she wanted him to be in a school where "getting good grades is cool" and where he would be encouraged to hold high expectations for himself, which did not appear likely in the organized program for deaf and hard of hearing students he was in. Although he loves school, like many deaf young people, Robbie does not particularly enjoy school tasks, particularly reading and writing. However, he is an avid reader of newspapers—especially the sports page—and spends a lot of time at the computer, where he purposefully reads and writes.

From my year in second grade with Tom, Robbie, and Paul, I learned several important lessons. First was the embarrassment of the uninitiated when I inadvertently sat in the "bad kid's" chair outside the principal's office and then when I unwittingly stood in the lunchroom in the spot where the misbehavers were simultaneously isolated and put on display. Once enlightened, I could focus on the really important lessons that Tom, Robbie, Paul, Ms. Roberts, Ms. Adams, and Mrs. Hart taught me. I learned that children and adults can use ASL to discuss many topics. Surprisingly, even English, reading, and writing can be discussed using ASL. ASL is undoubtedly an appropriate, useful, and efficient medium of instruction, a fact that comes as no surprise to generations of deaf students who attended residential secondary schools.

The second lesson learned is that a medium of instruction must be put to an instructional purpose. That is, school for deaf children should be regarded as education first. It may also be a political or legal endeavor, and it may also set the stage for social and civic improvement in future generations. However, first deaf children must be seen as genuine students who go to school to learn basic skills and to discover how to use their growing abilities and knowledge to continue learning through elementary, middle, high school, and beyond. A social contract is implicit in schools, and the same contract holds for the education of deaf students. Out of respect for deaf children and their intellectual and linguistic potential, their schooling must be seen as an educational endeavor. As other researchers in the deaf education world have observed, placement decisions,

References

Allen, T. 1986. Patterns of academic achievement among hearing impaired students: 1974 and 1983. In *Deaf children in America,* ed. A. Schildroth and M. Karchmer. San Diego: College-Hill Press.

Allen, T., and T. Osborn. 1984. Academic integration of hearing impaired students. Demographic, handicapping, and achievement factors. *American Annals of the Deaf* 129:100–13.

Antia, S. 1982. Social interaction of partially mainstreamed hearing-impaired children. *American Annals of the Deaf* 137:381–88.

Banks, J. 1994. *All of us together.* Washington, D.C.: Gallaudet University Press.

Brill, R. 1978. *Mainstreaming the prelingually deaf child.* Washington, D.C.: Gallaudet College Press.

CADS. 1992–1993. Inclusion statistics: 1992–1993 Annual Survey. Website, Center for Assessment and Demographic Studies. Washington, D.C.: Gallaudet University.

Cazden, C. 1988. *Classroom discourse: The language of teaching and learning.* Portsmouth, N.H.: Heinemann.

Cole, M., and S. Cole. 1993. *The development of children,* 2d. ed. New York: Scientific American Books.

Commission on Education of the Deaf. 1988. *Toward equality: Education of the deaf.* Washington, D.C.: U.S. Government Printing Office.

Donaldson, M. 1978. *Children's minds.* New York: W. W. Norton and Co.

Dyson, A. 1989. *Multiple worlds of child writers: Friends learning to write.* New York: Teachers College Press.

———. 1991. The word and the world: Reconceptualizing written language development or, Do rainbows mean a lot to little girls? *Research in the Teaching of English* 25:97–123.

———. 1994. The Ninjas, the X-men, and the ladies: Playing with power and identity in an urban primary school. *Teachers College Record* 96:219–39.

Ferreiro, A., and A. Teberosky. 1982. *Literacy before schooling.* Portsmouth, N.H.: Heinemann.

Furth, H. 1973. *Deafness and learning.* Belmont, Calif.: Wadsworth Publishing Co.

Gearhart, B., R. Mullen, and C. Gearhart. 1993. *Exceptional individuals: An introduction.* Pacific Grove, Calif.: Brooks/Cole Publishing Co.

Gustason, G., D. Pfetzing, and E. Zawolkow, eds. 1972. *Signing Exact English.* Los Alamitos, Calif.: Modern Signs Press.

Halliday, M. 1975. Learning how to mean. In *Foundations of language development,* vol. 1, ed. E. Lenneberg and E. Lenneberg. New York: Academic Press.

Heath, S. 1978. *Teacher talk: Language in the classroom.* Washington, D.C.: Center for Applied Linguistics.

Higgins, P. 1990. *The challenge of educating together deaf and hearing youth: Making mainstreaming work.* Springfield, Ill.: Charles C. Thomas.

Holt, J. 1995. Classroom attributes and achievement test scores for deaf and hard of hearing students. *American Annals of the Deaf* 139:430–37.

Kluwin, T., and D. Moores. 1985. The effect of integration on the mathematics achievement of hearing-impaired adolescents. *Exceptional Children* 52:153–60.

Lane, H., R. Hoffmeister, and B. Bahan. 1996. *A journey into the deaf-world.* San Diego: DawnSign Press.

Large, D. 1980. Special problems of the deaf under the Education for All Handicapped Children Act of 1975. *Washington University Law Quarterly* 58:213–75.

Moores, D. 1996. *Educating the deaf: psychology, principles, and practices,* 4th ed. Boston: Houghton Mifflin.

Moores, D., and T. Kluwin. 1986. Issues in school placement. In *Deaf children in America,* ed. A. Schildroth and M. Karchmer. San Diego: College-Hill Press.

Nelson, K. 1985. *Making sense: The acquisition of shared meaning.* New York: Academic Press.

Padden, C. In press. The ASL lexicon. *International Review of Sign Linguistics.*

Padden, C., and C. Ramsey. 1996. Deaf children as readers and writers. Final project report to the U.S. Department of Education.

Padden, C., and T. Humphries. 1988. *Deaf in America: voices from a culture.* Cambridge, Mass.: Harvard University Press.

Padden, C., and R. Tractenberg. In press. Intended and unintended consequences of educational policy for deaf children. University of California at San Diego: Research Program in Language and Literacy.

Ramsey, C. 1984. American values in a Deaf American life. Master's thesis, Gallaudet University.

———. 1993. A description of classroom language and literacy learning among deaf children in a mainstreaming program. Ph.D. diss., University of California, Berkeley.

———. 1994. The price of dreams. In *Implications and complications for deaf students of the full inclusion movement,* ed. O. Cohen and R. C. Johnson. Gallaudet Research Institute Occasional Paper 94–102. Washington, D.C.: Gallaudet University.

———. 1996. Where is Deaf culture in the classroom? Working paper. University of California at San Diego: Research Program in Language and Literacy.

———. In press. Deaf children as literacy learners. In *A handbook for literacy educators: Research on teaching the communicative and visual arts,* ed. J. Flood, S. B. Heath, and D. Lapp. New York: Macmillan.

Ramsey, C., and C. Padden. In press. Natives and newcomers. *Anthropology and Education Quarterly.*

Saur, R., C. Layne, E. Hurley, and K. Opton. 1986. Dimensions of mainstreaming. *American Annals of the Deaf* 131:325–30.

Schein, J. D. 1996. The demography of deafness. In *Understanding deafness socially,* 2d ed., ed. P. Higgins and J. Nash. Springfield, Ill.: Charles C. Thomas.

Schildroth, A. 1988. Recent changes in the educational placement of deaf students. *American Annals of the Deaf* 133:61–67.

Schildroth, A., and S. Hotto. 1995. Race and ethnic background in the annual survey of deaf and hard of hearing children and youth. *American Annals of the Deaf* 140:96–99.

Scruggs, T., and M. Mastropieri. 1996. Teacher perceptions of mainstreaming/inclusion, 1958–1995: A research synthesis. *Exceptional Children* 63(1): 59–74.

Stack, K. 1996. The development of a pronominal system in the absence of a natural target language. Poster presented at Theoretical Issues in Sign Language Research, September, at McGill University, Montreal, Canada.

Stainback, W., S. Stainback, and G. Bunch. 1989. A rationale for the merger of regular and special education. In *Educating all students in the mainstream of regular education,* ed. W. Stainback, S. Stainback, and M. Forest. Baltimore, Md.: Paul H. Brookes Publishing Co.

Stubbs, M. 1980. *Language and literacy: The sociolinguistics of reading and writing.* London: Routledge and Kegan Paul.

Supalla, S. 1986. *Manually Coded English: The modality question in signed language development.* Master's thesis, University of Illinois at Champaign-Urbana.

Vygotsky, L. 1962. *Thought and language.* Cambridge, Mass.: MIT Press.

———. 1978. *Mind in society: The development of higher psychological processes,* ed. M. Cole, V. John-Steiner, S. Scribner, and E. Souberman. Cambridge, Mass.: Harvard University Press.

Wertsch, J. 1989. A sociocultural approach to mind: Some theoretical considerations. In *Sociocultural approaches to mind. Cultural processes, 2,* ed. J. Wertsch. 140–61.

Winston, E. 1992. Mainstream interpreting: An analysis of the task. In *The challenge of the 90s: New standards in interpreter education. Proceedings of the Eighth National Convention of the Conference of Interpreter Trainers,* ed. L. Swaby, 51–68.

Woodward, J. 1973. Some observations on sociolinguistic variation and American Sign Language. *Kansas Journal of Sociology* 9:191–200.

Woodward, J., T. Allen, and A. Schildroth. 1988. Linguistic and cultural role models for hearing-impaired children in elementary school programs. In *Language learning and deafness*, ed. M. Strong. Cambridge: Cambridge University Press.

Index

Academic subjects, 47, 57, 111
  in the mainstream classroom, 47,
    57
  in the self-contained classroom, 111
Accessibility of education, 45–47
American Sign Language (ASL)
  deaf students
    literacy skills attained through
      using, 24, 78, 111
    preference for pure signs over
      English-influenced ones, 103
  differences from English, effect on
    achieving literacy, 88–89
  lack of access to, effect on deaf chil-
    dren's education, 10
  as language of instruction, 20, 94–
    95, 115
  self-contained classroom's use of,
    77–78, 84–85, 111
  teachers' knowledge of, 16
Arithmetic, 28, 47, 65, 67
Art instruction, 65–66
ASL. *See* American Sign Language
Aspen School, 2, 13–25, 43–44. *See
    also* Mainstreaming; Methodol-
    ogy of study; Peer interaction;
    Self-contained classrooms
  deaf children's behavior, 44–45
  deaf students in, 13–15, 32, 47
  classroom teachers' experience, 42–
    43, 53–54
  communication at, 57–63
  interpreters, 45–47
  issues of contention, 56
  LRE implementation, 51–52
  placement decisions, 43–44,
    109–10
  self-contained classroom teachers,
    44, 52–53, 54–55

staff perceptions of mainstreaming,
    38–42, 47–51
Attitudes
  toward deaf students, 26, 39–42,
    48–49, 52–53, 59–60
  toward mainstreaming, 31, 37–46,
    55–57, 64, 77
  toward self-contained classrooms,
    56
  toward signing, 46–47, 58
Audiovisuals used in teaching, 43, 61

Banks, J., 30
Bilingual/bicultural education of deaf
    students, 76
Book sharing/book reading, 81–85
Brill, R., 40

Calendar time, 19, 56
Cazden, C., 5
"Chalk-and-talk" teaching method,
    36, 46, 59
Child collectives, 71–72, 74
Child development theory, 5–12, 36
Civil rights of deaf students. *See* Equal-
    ity of education
Classroom communication. *See* Lan-
    guage in the classroom; Peer in-
    teraction
Code-signs, 85
Cole, M. and S. Cole, 11
Commission on Education of the Deaf
    Report (1988), 30–31
Communication breakdown in the
    mainstream class, 60–62
Communication, logistics of in Aspen
    School, 57–63
Consequences of mainstreaming,
    113–16

mainstreaming classroom compared
with, 2–3, 23, 75–78, 110–12
other languages, exposure to, 86–88
removal of students from mainstreaming classroom to, 44–45
teacher-student interaction, 79–81,
86–92
teachers' views, 52–57, 75–77
Signing
communication vehicle needed by
deaf students, 36, 57
deaf students signing to themselves,
93–97, 102, 106
hearing students' competence,
68–74
instruction for hearing students, 68
other languages' use of signs, 86
teachers' attitudes toward, 46–47,
58
Signing Exact English (SEE), 6
Social development, 3–12, 36–37
Social interaction, 11. *See also* Peer
interaction
mainstreaming programs, 36–37, 92
self-contained classroom students,
78–79, 92
Social science. *See* Academic subjects
Sociohistorical theory, 3–5
Speaking by deaf students, 96
Spelling, assistance with, 101

Story reading, 81–85
Students, deaf. *See* Deaf students

Teachers
"chalk-and-talk" teaching method,
36, 46, 59
conflict between teachers of deaf
and mainstreaming teachers,
51–57
mainstreaming
attitude toward, 31, 37–45, 52–
64, 77
burden placed on teacher, 57–63
interpreter-teacher relationship,
46, 58–63, 65–66
student-teacher interaction,
65–66
training for, 30–31, 53, 62, 110
methodology of study, 14–16
self-contained classrooms, 52–57,
75–78
teacher training, 76
Transitions between subjects/activities,
66

Videotaping, 17–22
Vygotsky, L., 4, 7–9, 11, 73, 93

Winston, E., 61
Writing. *See* Journal writing